PORSCHE

PORSCHE

Power, Performance, and Perfection

Susann Miller

MALLARD PRESS

A FRIEDMAN GROUP BOOK

Published by MALLARD PRESS
An Imprint of BDD Promotional Book Company, Inc.
666 Fifth Avenue
New York, N.Y. 10103

Mallard press and the accompanying duck logo are registered
trademarks of BDD Promotional Book Co., Inc. Registered in the
U.S. Patent and Trademark Office.

ISBN 0-7924-5759-5

PORSCHE: Power, Performance, and Perfection
was prepared and produced by
Michael Friedman Publishing Group, Inc.
15 West 26th Street
New York, New York 10010

Editor: Dana Rosen
Art Direction: Devorah Levinrad
Designer: Kevin Ullrich
Photography Editor: Ede Rothaus

Typeset by Classic Type, Inc.
Color separations by United South Sea Graphic Art Co.
Printed and bound in Hong Kong by Leefung-Asco Printers Ltd.

DEDICATION

To all the men in my life: my father, my son, and my significant other.

ACKNOWLEDGMENTS

The New York offices of the Michael Friedman Publishing Group, Inc. have a fantastic staff who edited my manuscript and researched all the photography. Thank you Dana Rosen and Ede Rothaus.

There are many special thanks that go to my family, whom I neglected when I locked myself up in my computer room. The cat was fed because she jumped on the computer keys when she was hungry. I got fed because my stomach made strange noises. Everyone else had to fend for themselves.

I would like to thank Katrin Müller in the press department of Porsche AG in Germany, who looked through the archives for the early photos of Porsche history. The people at Porsche Cars North America, Inc. in Reno, Nevada, especially Bob Carlson in the racing division and Dan Hopper, deserve a big thank you for their help checking the many early dates and racing wins. Another thank you goes to Ed Triolo, whom I have known for over twelve years, beginning when I started working on my first Porsche book and Porsche magazine. Hal Williams deserves a special mention because he gave me this project in the first place. Many thanks go to Patti Reynolds for her assistance in reading a manuscript about a car she knew nothing about; to Tim Kuser, who taught me how to collect bits and pieces of Porsche collectibles; to Sandy Wagner for her laser printer and crazy jokes that kept us all slightly sane; and to John Kelly, who put up with it all. And last but not least, a thank you to Mom, who knows nothing about cars but who taught me to drive and made me what I am today!

CONTENTS

INTRODUCTION

This book is for the world's automobile enthusiasts. It is especially devoted to the Porsche lover, the Porsche "nut" (of which I am one), and the Porsche competitor, both on and off the track.

In any general automotive book found in the library, a bookstore, or even your own collection, the name Ferdinand Porsche will always be found in the index. He is mentioned as one of the greatest automotive engineers of all time, along with Marc Birkigt, Ettore Bugatti, Paul Daimler, Ernest Henri, Henry Leland, Colin Chapman, and Frederick Lanchester, to name but a few. Dr. Porsche designed the Austro-Daimler, the Auto Union Grand Prix cars, the Volkswagen, and various German army tanks during World War II. He worked on projects for Wanderer (now part of Audi), Citroën, Alfa-Romeo, Volvo, Fiat, and the list goes on. All this occurred before the first Porsche sports car was built. He also designed airplane engines, fire trucks, and even tractors. Few today are aware to whom we have to be thankful for helping us to go fast, faster, fastest!

For the first-time buyer of a Porsche book:

- Did you know that there really is a Porsche family and that they are still very much a part of the Porsche automobile manufacturing company in Stuttgart-Zuffenhausen, Germany?

For both the new and old Porsche lover:

- Did you know that Porsche is pronounced as a two-syllable word: "Por'-sha", not "Porsh"?
- Did you know that the design firm of Porsche (at the Weissach Development Center) in Germany devotes most of its energies to outside contracts? More than 32 percent of Porsche's labor force works on outside research and development for automotive, motorcycle, technological, and aerodynamic corporations all over the world, including the automotive industry in the United States?

So much has been written about Porsche throughout the world that it would be very difficult to develop a book that is all new. But whether you are a first-time Porsche-book buyer/collector or a long-time Porsche enthusiast, this book will be enjoyable and educational. It is a book you will refer to many times and keep in your library forever.

Weissach Development Center.

Ten Porsche Milestone Projects Before the 356

1900–1903	**Electric Car**	The Lohner-Porsche, a gasoline engine generating electricity for front-wheel drive hub motors.
1910	**Austro-Daimler**	Wins first, second, and third places in Prince Henry Trials.
1914–1918	**"Land Train"**	Used during World War I to tow heavy artillery on land or rail; gasoline engine generator with hub-mounted motors on each trailer.
1923	**Austro-Daimler**	Post-World War I, type M, 6-cylinder.
1924–1928	**Mercedes-Benz**	2.0-liter, 4-cylinder supercharged Mercedes wins Targa Florio; development of 6-cylinder S models that lead to the famed SSK.
1934–1939	**Auto Union**	6.3-liter, V–16 rear engine Grand Prix car exceeded 170 mph (272 kph) (1934), 180 mph (288 kph) (1935); V–12 in 1938. Two world records not broken for twenty years.
1935–1939	**Volkswagen**	"The People's Car," commissioned by Chancellor Hitler of the Third Reich, a project for an inexpensive, all-purpose vehicle.
1939	**Land Speed Record Car**	44-liter, 3,000 bhp Daimler-Benz aero engine, 6-wheel land speed record car designed to travel 400 mph (644 kph); 2.8 tons (2.5 metric tons), 29 feet (8.7 m) long. World War II interrupted final developments.
1940–1944	**Tiger Tank**	56 tons (51 metric tons); gasoline-electric power, full armor, and mobile guns.
1942–1945	**Maus (mouse) Tank**	189 tons (171 metric tons); largest tank in World War II. Gasoline-electric power; only prototypes were built.

356 Speedster.

IT STARTED AS A DREAM

Ferdinand Porsche was born on September 3, 1875, in Bohemia (now part of Czechoslovakia) and passed away on January 30, 1951.

EARLY PROJECTS BEFORE THE PORSCHE AUTOMOBILE

From his early childhood, Ferdinand Porsche was interested in experimenting with electricity. In 1895, at the age of nineteen, after working as an apprentice for a year, he became an electrical technician in Vienna, Austria. At this time, motorcars were slowly appearing throughout the world, beginning as a rich man's toy.

In 1898, Porsche joined Lohner and Company, a carriage-making firm turned automobile manufacturer,

and he began designing and building electric-powered cars. At the Universal Exposition in Paris in 1900, the first Lohner-Porsche was exhibited. It was fitted with electric hub motors that drove the front wheels and could reach speeds of close to 25 mph (40 kph), a sure ticket-getter if it could be caught. Porsche was only twenty-five years old, and he already had his name on vehicles being driven on the roads.

By 1901, Porsche realized that to reach higher speeds and to get better performance, he would have to look at the gasoline engine. He conceived of an ingenious design for an automobile that contained both electricity and gasoline. The gasoline engine drove an electric generator that provided electricity for the motors in the wheels. If the gasoline engine broke down, the vehicle could still travel an additional thirty-five miles (56 km) to a safe overnight stop or back home using the electricity in its large storage battery.

In 1906, the Austrian branch of the Daimler Motor Co. offered the position of technical director (chief engineer) to the young Porsche. The biggest seller from the company at the time was a car called Mercedes, and within a short time its greatest competition, on both sides of the Atlantic, was a car from a company called Benz. Porsche

The Beginning of a Legend

The Porsche crest as we know it today was not designed until 1952. The early cars had only the Porsche lettering. The crest incorporates the Stuttgart coat of arms, showing a rampant black horse on a yellow background (the old area of Stuttgart had been a horse stud farm). The black and red colors with the six curved staghorns represent the crest of the state of Baden-Württemberg, and the Porsche name runs across the top.

continued to work on gasoline-electric cars, and in 1909 he developed his first aviation engine.

At this time, racing was becoming very important to the car-manufacturing communities. By 1910, Porsche devoted himself to winning the Prince Henry Trials for Austro-Daimler by using new streamlined designs for the exterior and an 86-bhp, 4-cylinder engine. The three cars Austro-Daimler entered won first, second, and third place, with Porsche driving the winning car. Between 1911 and 1914, two hundred of this winning model were sold.

During 1917, Porsche was awarded the title of Dr. Ing. honoris causa by the Vienna Technical Institute. Later, he would receive another honorary doctorate, in 1924, and the honorary title of professor, in 1940, both from the Technical University of Stuttgart.

During World War I, Porsche worked on designs for heavy transport vehicles to move military equipment on land and/or rail. His original hub-motor drive was used on flatbed trailers, with the wheels powered by individual hub motors. As many as ten trailers were attached and moved like a train, with a converted gasoline tractor as the engine generator.

Above: Ferdinand Porsche at the wheel of a gasoline-electric Lohner-Porsche at the Exelberg Hill Climb in 1902, where the car set a new record. His employer, Ludwig Lohner, sits next to him.

As the years passed after the war, Dr. Porsche continued to work for Austro-Daimler, designing and developing new cars for the street. He also designed and built a toy car for his eleven-year-old son, Ferry, which could reach speeds of 30 mph (48 kph) in the backyard.

Porsche continued to develop and design racing machines. During the early part of 1922, he designed the Sascha, a small sports car that competed in the Targa Florio in Sicily. The following year Porsche left the firm in Austria and moved to Daimler in Stuttgart, Germany, beginning development on supercharged cars. By 1924, the supercharged racing car he developed for Daimler won the Targa Florio at a record average speed of over 40 mph (64 kph) over the 67-mile (107-km) course. In 1926, Daimler and Benz merged.

During this period of his life, Porsche was very concerned about the size of the vehicles on the road, and he wanted to develop an economy car for the everyday driver. But Daimler-Benz had no interest in pursuing this idea, or the many other radical ideas that Dr. Porsche came up with, so he moved back to Austria to work for the Steyr group as chief engineer. He remained there for less than a year before Steyr started having financial problems. So in 1930, Dr. Porsche made one of the biggest decisions of his career: he decided to open his own independent design and engineering office. He moved his family back to Stuttgart, Germany, the automotive design center of Europe, taking some of his associates with him. The following year, the Porsche Konstruktionbüro für Motoren-Fahrzeug-Luftfahrzeug Und Wasserfahrzeugbau became a fully registered company specializing in engines, automobiles, aircraft, and ships. Dr. Porsche's son, Ferry, joined his father's firm at the age of twenty-one, after having studied as an apprentice with both Bosch and Steyr.

One of the first designs from the new company was a 2.0-liter car for the firm Wanderer. After 1932, Wanderer

At the 1922 Targa Florio, Alfred Neubauer sits behind the wheel of the new Austro-Daimler Sascha race car. The car's designer, Ferdinand Porsche, stands behind the "6." Two such cars swept the 1,100cc class. Unfortunately for Dr. Porsche, the company was not interested in such small cars, and he decided to leave.

From Number 7 to 968

It was decided early on that each project in the Porsche design offices would be assigned a job number in sequence. The job numbers would later become the model numbers of Porsche automobiles. The numbering started in 1930 with design number 7, the Wanderer car chassis. The engineers wanted the contracting company to think that the new Porsche company had past experience in design, hence the number 7 instead of 1. The Auto Union Grand Prix car was number 22. The Daimler-Benz land speed record car was number 80. The 11-horsepower diesel tractor was number 323.

From the first 7 through the latest 968, the numbers continue to increase and get better with age.

became a member of Auto Union AG along with Horch, D.K.W., and Audi. Racing cars were produced and raced under the group name Auto Union, but private cars continued to be marketed by the individual companies.

In 1932, the torsion-bar suspension system was developed. It was first used by Auto Union for racing cars and later used for the Volkswagen, then refitted for the Citroën and Alfa-Romeo, to name but a few. This same year, Porsche designed a 16-cylinder Grand Prix engine, which showed up later in the Auto Union race car. These Auto Union cars raced all through Europe from 1934 to 1939, with the first win at the Grand Prix of Germany and the next in Switzerland in 1934. Their first winning car had the engine located behind the driver and had a top speed of 170 mph (272 kph); by 1935 the top speed increased to 180 mph (288 kph). It set world speed

Above: Erich von Delius driving an Auto Union V-16 Grand Prix car in 1936. The fuel tank was in the center of the vehicle, directly behind the driver, to minimize the effects of weight loss due to fuel usage. Near left: The right front suspension of an Auto Union Grand Prix car. It was similar to the suspension of the newly developed Volkswagen. Far left: A cutaway drawing of the 1935 Auto Union V-16 engine. All thirty-two valves were operated from one centrally located camshaft. Dr. Porsche designed this engine to be light, and in a conservative rpm range.

records that took decades to break, and it was said to be the ugliest thing on four wheels, a hideous monstrosity. But it could win.

Also in the 1930s, Porsche was commissioned by the Third Reich to design the ultimate car for the people, an idea that Hitler had announced at the Berlin Motor Show of 1934, and a project that Porsche had always wanted to work on. The car had to be inexpensive and all-purpose. Porsche and his team built three prototypes in his own garage. The car was ultimately named the Volkswagen.

Right: Ferdinand Porsche at the rear of a very early Volkswagen. Notice the large sliding-cloth sunroof and the radio antenna centrally mounted above the windshield. Below: The cockpit area of the Daimler-Benz T80 land speed record car with all the bodywork removed. The steering wheel is cut off at the bottom to allow room for the driver's legs.

Although Porsche was very involved in the VW project, he continued working on designs for his own company, and he acted as technical chief of Auto Union's racing department until the end of 1937. One project that occupied his time was a monstrous 44-liter V–12 aero engine in a 29-foot (8.8-m) racer for Daimler-Benz, designed to challenge the world land speed record. The car was completed but never run because of the outbreak of World War II. This car, said to be capable of 405 mph (652 kph), can be seen today in the Mercedes-Benz museum in Stuttgart, Germany.

Porsche also found time to design an aerodynamic coupe version of the VW for the Berlin–Rome Rally, managing to complete three cars in 1939. Of the three cars, one has survived and was purchased from the Porsche family by the one-armed race driver, Otto Mathé, in the 1950s when funding for new Porsche projects was needed. This car was displayed at the Laguna Seca, California, historic races in 1982.

Between 1940 and 1944, Professor Porsche contributed to the German war effort by designing a multitude of tanks, including the Leopard, the Tiger, and the Maus (mouse), an impractical 189-ton (171-metric-ton) tank, the largest in World War II. Since the weight of this mammoth vehicle could collapse most bridges and roadways, a special rail car was to be built to transport it, but the war ended before the Maus saw any action.

During the war, the Porsche design and engineering studio moved all the designs, drawings, research, and archives to a converted sawmill in Gmünd, Austria, in order to save as much as possible if Stuttgart was ever bombed. By the end of the war, to keep fully operational, the company repaired farm equipment and war-time Volkswagens.

By 1945, Professor Porsche, his son Ferry, and the professor's son-in-law, Dr. Anton Piëch, were imprisoned by the French. Ferry Porsche was quickly freed, but Profes-

Above: The Daimler-Benz T80 land speed record car without its aluminum skin. It was intended to top 400 mph (640 kph) but never ran due to the outbreak of World War II. All four rear wheels are driven. Left: The Daimler-Benz T80 survived the war, but without its engine. The body was made by hand, with protruding side wings added for downforce and stability.

Under the leadership of Ferry Porsche, the son of the firm's founder, the first automobile with the name "Porsche" was built in the summer of 1948. This photograph was taken at the Porsche workshops at Gmünd in Kärnten province, Austria, where the company had been moved from its home in Stuttgart due to the war.

sor Porsche and Dr. Piëch were not released for almost two years. Under the direction of Professor Porsche's daughter, Louise Piëch, and later his son, Ferry, the company continued to survive.

During the rebuilding of the Porsche firm, they received a commission from an Italian industrialist to develop the Cisitalia (Type 360) for Grand Prix racing. This contract was perhaps the most important commission in Porsche history. The money that was advanced for the design work helped the firm get on its feet financially and supplied the funds used to pay the French government to release Professor Ferdinand Porsche and Anton Piëch. The car was designed by Ferry Porsche and his team for Formula 1 racing; it contained a water-cooled 12-cylinder engine, double overhead camshafts, twin superchargers, and four-wheel drive that could be disengaged at will. The engine was located in the rear behind the driver, and the car possessed a five-speed synchronized gearbox, an amazing feature considering it was

built in 1948. The car was designed to reach 385 horsepower at 10,600 rpm but was never tested. The backer ran out of money before the car ever raced in Formula 1 events (but it did race in later years in Argentina). Eventually, the car was purchased back by the Porsche family and has been fully restored. Today the Cisitalia can be seen at the Porsche museum in Stuttgart, Germany.

After the French were paid the bail needed to release the prisoners (the French later dropped all charges), Professor Porsche returned to Gmünd, Austria, to continue in the pursuit of his dream, to produce a car that would bear his name. This would become the Porsche 356.

By this time Porsche was a very sick man. When he celebrated his seventy-fifth birthday in September 1950, over three hundred Porsches had been produced and delivered to their happy buyers. He suffered a stroke and passed away in early 1951.

But the company was in good hands with his son, Ferry Porsche.

Little-Known Information

In 1952, Porsche was contracted by Studebaker, in South Bend, Indiana, to develop a new car and engine. This project helped Porsche acquire enough money to start construction on a new factory in Zuffenhausen, Germany, a suburb of Stuttgart.

Owning a Part of Porsche

Porsche was a family-owned company until 1972. The members of the family then became stockholders: Ferry Porsche, his sister, Louise Piëch, and their respective children, totaling ten persons, now each held ten percent of the company. A major change occurred in 1984 when one-third of the company's capital stock went on sale on the German stock exchange in the form of non-voting preferred shares. Then one-sixth of the family's privately owned stock was converted into nonvoting preferred shares so that family members could redeem some cash value if they so chose. When the stock was offered for sale, it sold out in three hours—many people wanted to be part of the Porsche legend.

Today, the members of the Porsche family are not directly involved in the management of Porsche AG, but Professor Ferry Porsche, Ferdinand Alexander Porsche, and Dr. Wolfgang Porsche are members of the board of directors.

Porsche Number 1

The first car to bear the Porsche name was a two-passenger, air-cooled, mid-engine 356 sports car. Based on Volkswagen components, it was a hand-built, aluminum-bodied open car, with a tubular space frame, and the engine mounted in front of the rear axle. All later 356s and 911s had the engine mounted behind the rear axle to provide more luggage space and room for an additional passenger. (The mid-engine mounting of that first car was not duplicated until 1953 with the 550 Spyder.) The VW 1.1-liter engine was modified to reach a top speed of over 84 mph (135 kph). It was first displayed to the motor press at the Swiss Grand Prix on July 4, 1948, to great reviews. The company had hoped to be able to produce five hundred cars. The rest is history: from 1948 to 1965 over 76,000 of these cars were produced.

This first Porsche 356/01 can be seen at the Porsche museum in Stuttgart.

Porsche Type 356, Number 1. Handmade in 1948, this car was a mid-engine roadster. The air-cooled, 1,131cc, 40 horsepower engine obtained its cooling air through the two long rows of oval vent openings that ran down either side of the rear deck lid. The "A" at the rear left stands for Austria. The "K" on the license plate stands for the province of Kärnten.

CHAPTER TWO

THE 356
(1948 TO 1965)

The birth of the 356 took place in Gmünd, Austria, in a drafty, decrepit, wooden sawmill. It sounds like the beginning of a religion, and that statement is close to being correct. Porsche collecting today appears to be on the fanatic level, at least among collectors having anything to do with the early automobiles such as the 356, and especially the Speedster.

In 1948, 1949, and early 1950, fewer than sixty hand-made, aluminum-bodied coupes were produced (only four were completed the first year). All the cars produced in Gmünd were hand hammered over a wooden buck, and most of the engine components were manufactured without a machine shop. When you hear ''made by hand,'' that was the truth. Many of the 356 parts, such as the braking system, engine, suspension, and transmission, were taken directly from the VW with special modifications. (This exchange with VW continues even through the 1990s.) Porsches were always designed for speed, as one

can see by the aerodynamic lines even in the early cars. The 356s were nothing like the other cars of that era and were looked upon as being unusual. These early cars were sold in Holland, Sweden, and Switzerland. In fact, it was Swiss backing that made the 356 possible. This was a very difficult time for any manufacturer: Europe was in ruins following the war and metal building materials were almost impossible to obtain.

The Porsche firm moved to Stuttgart, Germany, in 1950 and contracted with the coach-building firm of Reutter to produce the bodies for the new Porsches. The original plan was to have eight to nine bodies delivered a month, but to Porsche's surprise, it received so many advance orders that by the end of 1950, a total of 298 cars had been delivered. (By March 1954, a total of 5,000 Porsches had been produced.)

In late 1951, three engines were offered in the 356. The sales literature at the time touted an air-cooled, horizontally opposed 4-cylinder engine with overhead valves,

Page 20: A restored 1955 Porsche Speedster sitting in front of the former Guggenheim estate, now a park, in Sands Point, New York. Page 21: The seats of a racing GS/GT Speedster. Right: The side view of Porsche No. 1. The body was made entirely by hand at the Porsche workshop on the outskirts of the Austrian town of Gmünd. Most of the mechanical parts were taken directly from the Volkswagen. With its aluminum bodywork, the car weighed barely 1,300 pounds (585 kg).

mounted behind the rear axle. The hot engine for the day was the 1,500cc that had set new world's records at the high-banked track at Montlhery, France. The street car weight was only 1,640 pounds (745 kg), and with a heavy foot, a driver could reach a speed of close to 100 mph (161 kph)—not bad for 1951. As the speeds increased, so did the stopping power. Porsche always wanted to be sure the car could get out of any trouble. When the 1500 Super engine was offered in late 1952, a synchromesh transmission and 280mm brakes were new features. Another new addition was the convertible.

Racing was very important for Porsche, and awards were very high for its cars on both sides of the Atlantic. Some of the early sales brochures even listed all the racing results for that year.

In North America at this time, safety laws were changing, and any imported car had to meet regulations. One such adjustment was safety bumpers, called over-rider bars, or bows. Bumper guards were added to the Porsche's newly designed bumpers, which had been moved away from the body. The extra bars protected the body from the larger and heavier North American automobiles.

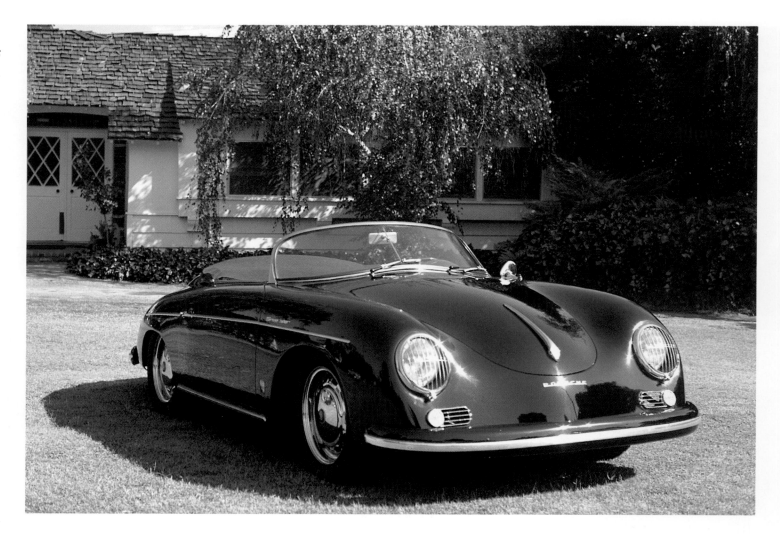

A beautifully restored 356A Speedster with brakes, chrome wheels, and hubcaps from a later 356C. The front bumper trim is a thin aluminum strip with no rubber insert, a stock item on Carreras. The early-style headlight grilles, a factory option, were designed to replace the thick glass covers.

In 1952, Porsche developed, for export only, the America Roadster, a joint idea between Porsche and its East Coast American distributor, Max Hoffman. Designed for U.S. buyers who wanted a car to race, it possessed an aluminum cabriolet body for lightness, and even had a removable windshield. The owner and friend could drive the car to the track, take off the extra weight (even the license plates), race, put everything back on, and return home. Of the sixteen Roadsters that were built, fourteen came to the United States to be sold to Porsche racing enthusiasts.

Porsches were selling all over Europe at this time. A special sales brochure in Swedish was developed for the new and growing market in Sweden. Brochures were

printed in 1953, 1956, and 1962 (an eight-page piece on the 356B). Volkswagen Canada Ltd. was marketing the Porsche in Canada and designing its own literature.

The hot sports cars in North America in 1953 were the Austin-Healey 100, the Triumph TR2, and the Corvette. Max Hoffman was having trouble selling Porsches, so he suggested that the factory strip down a car to get it below $3,000, but still keep it comfortable and able to be used for the street. This idea became the birth of the Speedster. The car's basic body was from the cabriolet, with a shortened windshield, a top with no lining, no roll-up windows (just side curtains in case of poor weather), and a bare-minimum interior. Except for the GS/GTs, all Speedsters had a thin chrome strip along the side from the front fender to the back (as did the later Convertible Ds and Roadsters). The Speedster was almost exclusively designed for and marketed in the United States, but the factory printed a price sheet that showed an early attempt to market the car for Germany. The overall look of the car gave it the nickname ''bathtub,'' a nickname that stands to this day. The Speedster weighed 150 pounds (68 kg) lighter than any other Porsche. The car was available in 1954 with a choice of two engines, and the price was perfect: $2,995, but you had to pay extra if you wanted a heater. Today, the car is one of the most sought after models for the street in the 356 line, bringing over $50,000 in many cases.

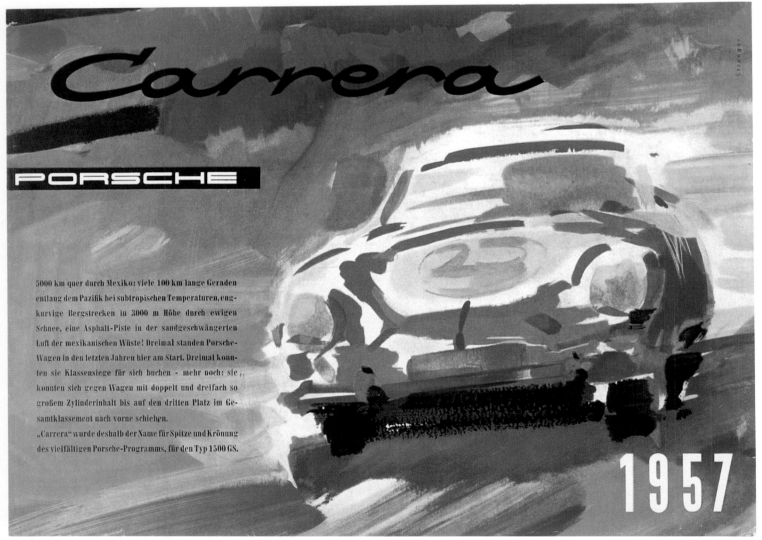

Top: This 1959 356A Carrera GT displays the optional removable late-style headlight grilles. Bottom: In 1957, Porsche created a special sales folder for its top-of-the-line Carreras named for the Carrera Panamericana (Pan-American Road Race) in Mexico, where Porsches performed extremely well. The Carreras used the famous race-bred 4-cam engine. In street trim, they produced 100 horsepower from 1,500cc.

The assembly line at Porsche, where 1955 cars are being finished. The two convertibles in the foreground are Speedsters, as are the three light-colored cars in the middle of the line. Engine assembly is taking place at the far right.

Also in 1954, Porsches were available with a choice of six different engine sizes: 1100 (dropped in late 1954), 1300, 1300A, 1300S, 1500, and 1500S. Only the two largest models were exported to North America. The 1500 model had no radio, rear folding seats, passenger sun visor, or adjustable passenger seatback. The 1500Super model possessed all of those features. There were three body styles: coupe, cabriolet (with roll-up windows and padded top), and Speedster. The coupe and cabriolet used the name "Continental" on the side of the car for 1955 in North America only.

Porsche was entering many races and adopted the Italian "Spyder" designation for the 550/1500RS, which it planned to place in limited production as a pure racing car for general sale with delivery late in 1954.

In 1955, the advertising slogans for the cabriolet described the car as the "Dior model of the Porsche family" and "The car women sigh over."

The 356A

The Frankfurt Auto Show, an event held in odd-numbered years, was the place to introduce new models to the public to review in the 1950s, as it still is today. At the Frankfurt Auto Show in September 1955, Porsche introduced the new 356A models for 1956. The changes were very noticeable, including the new all-steel body, still produced by Reutter. The wheel size was decreased from 16 to 15 inches. But the most noticeable change to the exterior was the curved windshield. The interior started to be truly plush, with a new gas gauge for the not so daring. A new transmission was also introduced. The 356 Carrera/1500GS was also unveiled at this time, and by 1957 two versions were offered—one intended for competition and the other for maximum comfort and performance combined.

Top: *An option on Porsches in the late 1950s and early 1960s was chrome knock-off wheels. Safety regulations did not allow the usual two or three "ears" used to "knock off" the large center wheel nuts, so a special wrench had to be carried for this purpose. Although quicker to remove, these wheels were considerably heavier than the standard ones. Bottom: The two small round taillights used at either side of Porsches from 1952 through early 1957 are called "Beehive" lights, due to their shape. Opposite page: A late 356B Porsche stripped and modified for hill climbs.*

Wonderful accessories were offered the Porsche customers, including a matching set of fitted luggage for the back seat with special straps to hold everything in place, and even a small bag to fit in the front luggage space behind the spare tire, available in leather or plaid. The most unusual option was a bench seat for the front instead of the two bucket seats. The advertisements read: "A perfect solution to the problem of where to put Junior."

The Convertible D was introduced in the summer of 1958 for the 1959 model year only. Called the "Speedster D" in preproduction publicity, the "D" came from the builder of the body, Drauz of Heilbronn, near Stuttgart. Considered a more comfortable and upgraded car than the Speedster, this convertible had roll-up windows, a higher top with a large rear window, coupe seats, and windshield washers as standard equipment. By the following year, the Speedster was no longer available; only the Convertible D and the luxury open car earlier called the cabriolet were shown in sales literature of the day. It should also be pointed out that the firm of D'Ieteren Freres in Brussels, Belgium, produced the Roadster body for Porsche from early 1961 to early 1962. The firm of Karmann produced a cabriolet with a fixed hardtop ("notchback") from 1961 through 1962.

THE 356B

At the Frankfurt Auto Show in September of 1959, Porsche unveiled the 356B for the 1960 model year with the new T-5 body and a "souped up" Super 90 engine. The bumpers were raised to give the car even more protection.

In 1961, the T-6 body was introduced for the 1962 model year delivery. The front hood was squared off, making it easier to load the trunk. A few added details included an enlarged windshield and rear window for the coupe and cabriolet hardtop. The gas tank was rede-

This page: *Details from a restored 1955 Type 356 Speedster. The grille alongside the turn signal (top left) is to allow the horn to be heard. The grille on the rear deck lid (top right) allows air to cool the engine; there is no other point of access. The "Speedster" name (bottom), plated with 18K gold, was attached to the side of each front fender.* Opposite page: *First introduced at the end of 1954 for the 1955 model year, the Speedster was a lighter-weight, no-frills Porsche convertible made to sell in the American market.*

Bottom left: *An Erich Strenger illustration of an early Type 356, used for a sales brochure. Top right: A view through the two grilles in the rear deck lid of a Type 550 Spyder. The spare tire, a requirement during endurance races, was strapped to special saddles atop the transaxle. Bottom right: The bodies of Porsches were manufactured by outside firms through the 1960s. Each company affixed its own badge to the lower right front fenders. This picture shows the badge of D'Ieteren Brothers in Belgium.*

signed to allow more room in the luggage compartment, and the fuel filler cap for the gasoline was now in the right front fender with an inside release, so the driver no longer had to open the trunk to fill the tank. All models now had an electric clock, and the double grille on the engine compartment cover was now standard. (The twin grilles otherwise appeared on America Roadsters, Spyders, and some "A" Carreras.) The two-tone rear-view mirror was introduced. With a touch of a button, it cut out the glare of the headlights of vehicles coming from behind at night. Also new was a variable speed windshield-wiper system. The T-6-B stayed in production for only two years, 1962 and 1963, when the new C model became ready for production.

The Carrera 2 was introduced in September 1961, but did not go into production until April 1962. The power plant was a descendant of the Spyder engine—a real quickie, which produced 130 horsepower from its two liters. Available in a coupe and a cabriolet, only one hundred cars were originally planned for production, but the final total was more than 450, some of which were built on the later 356C chassis.

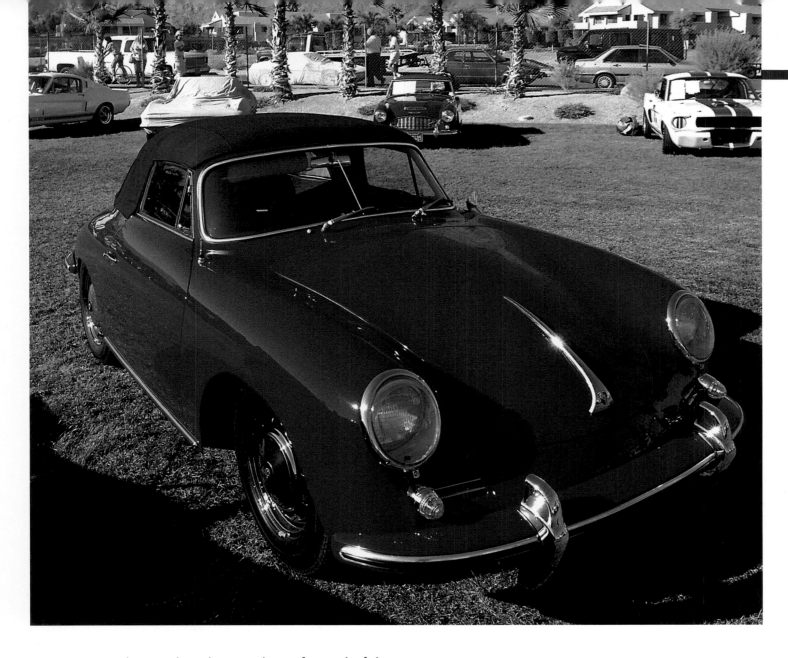

Again, Porsche produced a number of wonderful accessories for the 356, one of which was whitewall tires. Another very rare item was an electric sunroof for the detachable top. The rarest of all, and one that was probably lost forever, was a plastic suitcase for the Roadster that fit over the tunnel hump in the back.

In Thun, Switzerland, the custom coachbuilder Beutler produced a four-passenger coupe. It was truly a four-seater. The rear seats could be folded down separately to give more space, and there was even an area behind the rear seats for luggage. A small number of these cars were produced in 1962 using the 356B chassis; on occasion one will show up at a car show today.

THE 356C

During July 1963, the first 356C model was being introduced for the 1964 model year. One of the major advertising details emphasized the new four-wheel disc brakes, which had been used exclusively on race cars up to then. Three engines were available: the 1600C, the 1600SC, and the Carrera 2. A quote from the U.S. brochure of the time stated: ''We spent years developing a great competition car so you can have fun driving to work.'' Most of the sales brochures were printed in Germany in the language of the country they were to be shipped to, using the same photographs. The accessory

Top: *An excellent restoration of a 1965 Porsche 356SC coupe. The SC was offered in 1964 and 1965. At 95 horsepower, it was the most powerful of the pushrod-engine Porsches. Starting in 1964, disc brakes were standard on all Porsches.* Bottom: *The interior of the 1965 356SC. The optional wood-rimmed steering wheel is a much sought-after accessory.*

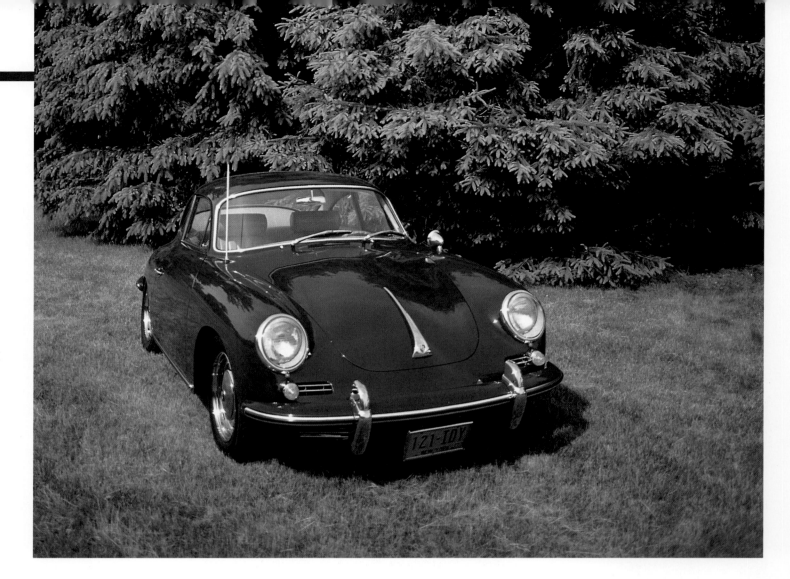

catalog was usually very detailed, with more than twenty-five pages, so it was not uncommon to see one printed in four languages: German, English, French, and Italian. On occasion, a local dealer produced a one-page handout and saved the more elaborate color brochure for more serious customers.

Production of the 356C officially ended in mid-September 1965. Porsche kept selling the SC in North America through the end of that year, even though the 356C was replaced by the 912 in the European market by April of that same year. Total production of all 356s exceeded 76,000 units.

The 901 was first introduced at the Frankfurt Auto Show in September 1963, but only one prototype car had been built for the show. The new car went into production in late 1964 as a 911: a new era had begun.

Porsche on the Ground and in the Clouds

During the 1950s, the Porsche design studios were involved with new ideas for vehicles used on land, water, and even in the air. Porsche engines were manufactured for a snow tractor, farm tractors with multiple-sized engines (one is on display at the Weissach test center), fire-engine pumps, and even a power-boat engine. The Porsche engine was always known to be reliable, so much so that it could be used in the air: starting in the 1910s, Professor Porsche designed aircraft engines. In the 1950s, Porsche built an airplane engine based on the 356 1.6-liter that could also be mounted vertically for helicopter use. During the early 1960s, Porsche developed and marketed an engine for a small one-man rescue helicopter.

By 1983, work was in progress for the PFM 3200, which was the aviation version of the 911 Carrera engine. One of the major differences between the land-based model and the aero design was that the camshafts were gear-, rather than chain-driven. The flight testing took place in a Cessna 182, and graduated to the Mooney. It was possible to order a Mooney with the Porsche aero engine, which reached 217 horsepower and had the standard twin spark plugs and dual electronic ignition found on all aircraft. A plus for the new Porsche aero engine was the design for the fuel mixture: a single power lever, rather than the three controls found on light aircraft, regulated the throttle, fuel/air mixture, and propeller.

The Mooney PFM 3200 was the ultimate Porsche for the high-flying car collector's garage.

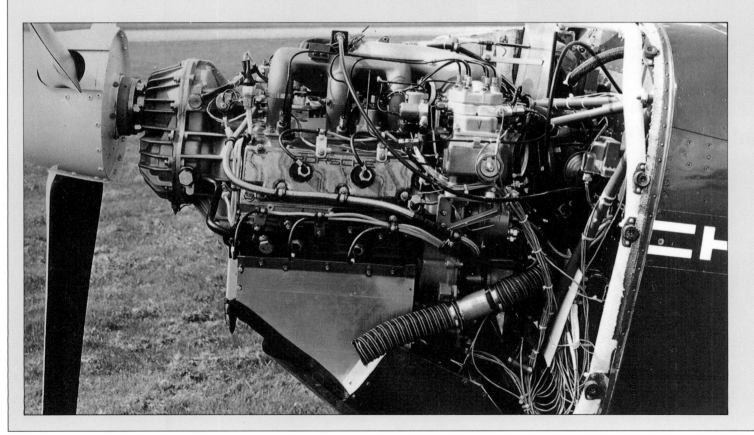

Porsche PFM 3200 installed in a Cessna 182 aircraft. Based on the 3.2-liter, 6-cylinder engine used in the 911 Carrera, it made flying easier and more enjoyable through the use of only a single control.

The first 901 was seen in 1963. Since then, the body style has seen improvements, but it has always been a little at a time. The car was renamed the 911, the lines have been lowered, the bumpers made larger, and the lights improved for better visibility, but the same basic design of the 1960s is still on the road in the 1990s. Today, the early 911s and 912s are in the price range of both collectors and drivers who want an extra car for fun.

A Porsche is a Porsche and will remain so, but every year the question is always asked: how long will the factory keep on producing the 911? The answer to the question is always the same: as long as there are buyers, Porsche will continue to build it.

911/912

The Porsche factory considered replacing the 356 in the late 1950s. The body style was getting dated, and the 4-cylinder engine was reaching its maximum capacity.

The transition from the 356C to the 911 and 912 took longer than customers anticipated. The first showing of the new body style was at the Frankfurt Auto Show in 1963, but the first cars were not delivered for almost two years. During this waiting period, many changes occurred in the 901, ranging from steering and suspension improvements to small details on the exterior body panels.

By the Paris Auto Show in 1964, Porsche was ready to take orders on the new 901. During this time, Peugeot informed Porsche that it had the French trademark rights to the use of a "0" between two numbers on all production cars. Because the French market was very important to the German car maker, Porsche changed the designation from "901" to "911." However, the first sales brochures published in English, French, German, and Italian had already been shipped to the dealers, so

until the new brochures were reprinted with the 911 designation, the now-rare 901 brochures were given out.

Since Peugeot did not have racing cars, Porsche continued to number its competition cars using the "0," and the numbering system for parts continues to this day to use the 901 to indicate a part for an early 911.

By April of 1965, the 912 had replaced the 356C in Europe. The 912 used a slightly detuned version of the 356SC 4-cylinder engine, allowing greater low-end range and drivability. The price for the 912 was $4,065 in Germany, and $4,690 (American dollars) in North America, while the 911 was $5,475 and $6,490, making the 912 a bargain. This more reasonably priced Porsche was very important, for the higher-priced model might have forced many otherwise loyal 356 Porsche drivers to change to other brands when replacing their 356s.

The first full production year for the 900 series Porsche was 1966. Half of the production was exported to the United States, one quarter was sold in West Germany, and the rest was exported to other parts of the world. A total of 13,000 cars were built, 9,000 of them 912s.

The Targa was introduced to the Porsche lineup at the Frankfurt Auto Show in 1965 for the customer that wanted a convertible-type vehicle. Called by Porsche "the world's first safety convertible" because of the brushed stainless steel roll bar, the Targa featured a vinyl-covered top that folded to fit into the trunk and a soft plastic rear window that zipped out; in 1968 a hard window for the Targa was available as an option for both the 911 and 912 models. The 911S (Super) was also new that year, with a top speed of 140 mph (224 kph); if the engine was driven too fast, a governor engaged to prevent internal damage.

Each year new options were available, and by 1968 you could order a sunroof for the coupe. This was also the year that the United States and Canada started extensive federal regulation on emissions and safety

standards, and Porsche was forced to make changes in its engines. Thus the 911S was discontinued in North America and would not be reintroduced until 1969.

In addition to the 912 and the standard 911, the 911L (Luxury) was available at a higher price (although the "S" was no longer available in North America, it was sold to the rest of the world). It was the first model year for the 2.0-liter 911T (Touring), which remained Porsche's low-end 911 for six years; it did not come to North America until the 1969 model year.

Also in 1968, the Sportomatic gearbox (not available on the 912 or 911S) was introduced. This option was important to the American market, where standard transmissions were generally not very popular. It was a normal Porsche four-speed transmission, but it was connected to the engine by a torque converter incorporating a regular clutch controlled by two microswitches at the bottom of the shift lever. There was no clutch pedal, but it did require some shifting for high performance. To shift,

all the driver had to do was touch the gearshift knob, thus disconnecting the transmission from the engine and allowing the next gear to be selected. However, the driver or passenger had to be careful not to touch the gearshifter unintentionally or the transmission would be suddenly out of gear.

After the 912 was dropped from the line at the end of its model year in 1969 to make way for the 914s (to fill the price gap below the 911), the only available Porsches were the 911T, the 911E (the mid-priced model), and the 911S. The yearly worldwide production figures were just under 15,000, which also included the last 912s.

The recession hit the car market in the early 1970s. Production figures for Porsche were down to just over 10,000 cars, and a few changes were occurring in the U.S. dealer showrooms. Whereas Volkswagen and Porsche dealers had been operating out of one facility, now new Porsche + Audi dealerships arose and had to operate in separate buildings from Volkswagen.

In 1972, the top Porsche engine size was up to 2.4 liters, more to improve emissions than to increase the power level. The chairman of the board of Porsche AG was Professor Ernst Fuhrmann; he believed that racing was good advertising, and the sales literature of the day projected such. The Porsche factory introduced the Carrera, officially called the "2.7-liter 911 Carrera RS," and made available after modifications to the competition customer as the "RSR." This car was the ultimate fast beast. Built in ultra-lightweight form, it weighed under 2,117 pounds (953 kg) and could reach 155 mph (249 kph) with unbelievable acceleration (0 to 60 mph [96.5 kph] in under six seconds). At 210 horsepower on regular gas, it was the most powerful production car in Germany. As it did not meet North American emission standards for the street, it was sold as a street car only in Europe, but it raced on both sides of the Atlantic. Besides going fast, it looked fast, with its "ducktail" rear spoiler, wide fender flares, and frontal

A 1970 911T. Beginning with the 1969 model year, Porsche lengthened the wheel base by moving the rear wheels back about 2 inches (47 mm), a change which improved the car's balance. Also in 1969, Porsche introduced fuel injection to the 911E and 911S models. In 1970, they enlarged all 911 engines by ten percent (to 2.2 liters).

Top: A 1970 911E Targa. The roof can be removed, folded, and carried in the trunk. Bottom left: The "Targa" name was given to the convertible version of the 911 in honor of Porsche's many victories in the now-discontinued Targa Florio open road race in Sicily. The brushed stainless steel band covers a functional roll bar. Bottom right: The interior of a 1970 911E Targa, showing the air conditioning ducts just under the dashboard and the Leatherette seats.

Cutaway view of the 930 Turbo engine.

Silver Anniversary 911S

In 1975, Porsche introduced a special edition, called the Silver Anniversary 911S, in honor of the twenty-fifth anniversary of the Porsche automobile. The car was offered worldwide as a limited edition in both the coupe and the Targa body design. They were all painted diamond-silver metallic with silver and blue-gray tweed fabric interiors. They had an embossed dash plaque on each car with Ferry Porsche's signature, and they were individually numbered starting with the number 2. A number 1 was never produced.

air dam for better handling. After many modifications to make it acceptable for highway use, the Carrera was finally introduced to the North American customer for street use (175 horsepower) in 1974.

Again, many new safety changes became mandatory for cars coming to North America. Since half of Porsche's production was coming to the United States, all necessary requirements were readily met, such as reinforcing the doors and adding heavy-duty bumpers to withstand a direct 5-mph (8-kph) impact. The production figures for the cars were again back up to the 15,000 mark by 1973. But in the early part of 1974, when the oil embargo hit, sales of Porsches fell 25 percent in North America and 50 percent in Europe. The Porsche factory went to a three-day workweek.

During this time, Porsche 914s and 924s were being sold along with the 911, and the 928 was being developed. The 911T was dropped, making the standard 911 the least expensive 911 model.

Then came the announcement of the 930 Turbo. Introduced in October of 1974, it was not available to the European market until March 1975, and the North American market had to wait until the 1976 model year. A most exciting Porsche, its turbocharged engine put out 260 horsepower at 5,500 rpm—it was said to be the dawn of a new era.

At the same time, the Carrera underwent a cosmetic change in its tail, from the racing-style ''ducktail'' to the ''whaletail'' competition-type spoiler that extended out with a rubber rim around the edge.

If the Porsche factory started to run out of a particular part close to the end of the model year and that part was to be changed for the next year, it was not uncommon to see the following year's updated part on that year's model. This was the case for the Carreras. Some customers received a late 1974 model with upgraded 1975 changes, such as new door handles, already installed.

In 1975, the emissions regulations in North America tightened even more. This forced Porsche to change the exhaust system, which decreased the horsepower by 10 in both the 911S and the Carrera. The changes required for the California cars reduced them an additional 5 horsepower. Porsche added new standard equipment and made a few price changes to its lineup for the North American market. With the company hoping to bring in more buyers, the new cars were priced lower than the year before. The plan seemed to work: in 1974, less than half the production was shipped to the United States and by late 1975, 55 percent was shipped.

The 1976 production year finally brought the 930 Turbo, later renamed the 911 Turbo, to North America as a Turbo Carrera, replacing the Carrera there. This car was the quickest, quietest, and fanciest high-performance street car Porsche had ever offered. It was said that the development alone amounted to over two million dollars. The developments Porsche had been perfecting for its racing cars were not wasted, for this was the most controllable turbocharged car of the day. The car was called "a dream car" by the press, and it competed with other exotics from Italy and England. The 930 Turbo had a sweeping rear wing, front spoiler, 7-inch-wide wheels at the front and 8-inch wheels at the rear, with flared fenders, tinted glass, power windows, power and electrically heated mirror, rear window wiper, headlight-washer system, fog lights, leather and plaid interior with velour carpeting, stereo radio with tape player, and air-conditioning. The performance was spectacular, with acceleration from 0 to

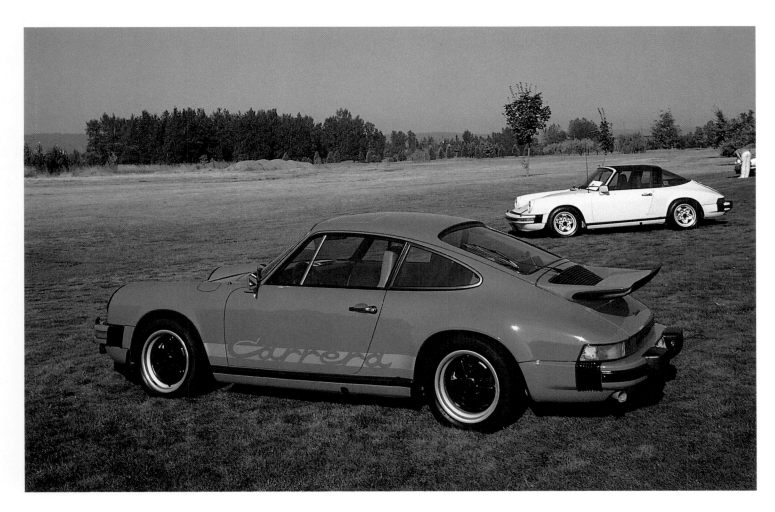

A 1975 911 Carrera, with the standard rear spoiler. In the background is a 911 Targa.

The 1976 912E was a limited edition model, introduced to fill the sales gap between the discontinued 914 and the soon-to-be introduced 924. With its lighter engine, the 912E was better balanced than a 911. On the street, the only way to distinguish between the models is by the "912E" emblem on that car's rear deck lid.

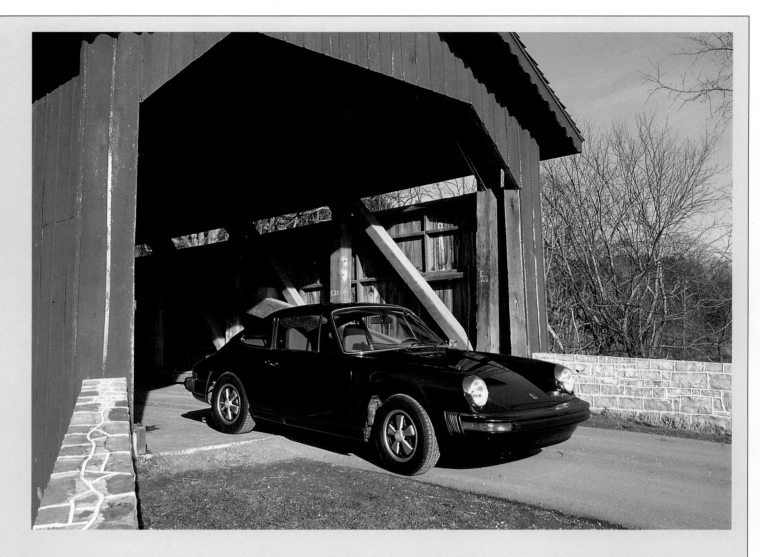

The 912E

The 912E developed out of Porsche's need for a car that could fill the gap between the discontinued 914 and the coming introduction of the 924, a car at the lower end of the Porsche market. Only slightly more than 2,000 912Es were produced in 1976 from available parts on hand. It was made with the basic 2.0-liter, 4-cylinder engine (from the discontinued 914) in a 911 body. The 912E was equipped with Bosch L-Jetronic fuel injection (the word for "fuel injection" in German is *Einspritzung*, hence the "E"), an air pump, and a pair of thermal reactors. The five-speed transmission was standard on this car.

The basic 911 body underwent a few changes to keep the price down. The brake rotors were not vented, and the tire-and-wheel combination was less than the 911. Even the interior was a little less fancy.

Optional equipment included an electric sunroof, limited-slip differential, forged alloy wheels, intermittent windshield wipers, and headlight washers. Also available were electric windows, a remote door mirror, air-conditioning, sports seats, fog lights, and tinted glass.

The owner's manual stated you could go from 0 to 60 mph (96.5 kph) in 13.5 seconds—not bad for a 4-cylinder!

60 mph (96.5 kph) in 5.7 seconds—an amazing feat for c street car!

By 1977, Great Britain and the United States were producing full-color deluxe editions of the Porsche sales catalogs, with supplemental pieces on the car radio equipment and tires. At this time, the only cars available in North America were the 911S and the 930 Turbo; the rest of the world had the 911, Carrera 3.0, and the Turbo. There was a choice of tires and wheels; if the softer compound was selected with a rating of 130 mph (208 kph), the car had a rev limiter added and the speedometer dial was marked. This option, called the "comfort group," included cruise control (not offered in Europe) and electric windows. The Turbo finally possessed a turbo boost gauge incorporated into the tachometer.

By the following year, the Turbo, with an enlarged engine, and the 911S underwent three price changes as the dollar fluctuated in Europe. This also was the year for the new 911SC, a slightly detuned version of the Euro-pean Carrera 3.0. It became the most desirable car for the Porsche enthusiast, with rear fender flares to incorporate a wider tire. The Sportomatic was now dropped from the options list.

Meanwhile, the emissions requirements in North America were getting very difficult for the 930 Turbo to meet. Porsche made the decision to stop exporting the car to North America after 1979. During August, when the production year changed to produce the 1980 cars, the Turbos were given the updated changes but were still sold as 1979 cars through December. This was the largest production year for the Turbo: 1,200 cars worldwide, with the last fifty given special numbered dash plaques and certificates stating that those cars were the last U.S. Turbos. However, they continued to be sold outside of North America.

In 1980, small changes that had been offered on the 911SC as options in previous years now became standard, such as the three-spoke, leather-covered steering

A 1977 911S coupe. Beginning with the 1974 models, Porsche restyled its cars to incorporate the new, stronger bumpers mandated by the North American safety regulations. The 911S was Porsche's basic 911 model in North America from 1975 through 1977.

The new 1978 6-cylinder models. The Turbo, in the foreground, underwent a ten-percent increase in engine size to 3.3 liters. The 911SC, in the background, had a 3.0-liter, 180 horsepower engine.

Left: *A 1980 Weissach Coupe, a limited edition 911 named for Porsche's research and development center near Stuttgart, Germany.* Following page: *A 1984 911 Targa. The "Carrera" name replaced the SC of previous years. On the track, the new Carrera accelerated from 0 to 60 mph (96.5 kph) in 6.2 seconds, with a top speed of 146 mph (234 kph).*

wheel, air-conditioning, and electric windows. This same year, a special edition 911SC Weissach Coupe was offered mid-year (see page 83). Only 400 cars were produced, with doric-beige leather interiors and contrasting burgundy piping on the seats, as well as burgundy carpeting with "911SC" burnished into the center. They were only available in two colors: black metallic and platinum metallic. This was also the year that the U.S. federal regulations would not let the speedometers read over 85 mph (137 kph), a decision reversed in 1982.

By 1981, Porsche introduced a berber tweed interior to the 911SC. The 3.0-liter engine continued to produce 172 horsepower, allowing the car to go from 0 to 60 mph (96.5 kph) in less than seven seconds. All the models throughout the world carried the seven-year anticorrosion warranty, which continued from owner to owner. The sunroof option was available, as well as a leather interior and 16-inch forged alloy wheels with low-profile tires. The right side mirror, electrically adjustable and heated, was an option, and it became standard equipment the following year along with leather front seats, headlight washers, power antenna, and rear speakers. The Targa was priced slightly higher than the coupe.

For the 1982 model year, the Porsche + Audi division of Volkswagen of America and Porsche AG heavily promoted the special program for vacation delivery that was much like the early days of the 356: the customer could order his or her car in North America with all the proper specifications and options and have it delivered to him or her in Europe. After driving around the continent, the customer returned it to the factory to be shipped back home across the Atlantic.

There were standard equipment additions on new cars in 1982 and, with the improved exchange rate, the price increase did not add up to the value of the new equipment, thus showing a net decrease in price in

Top: The 1984 Carrera engine was increased from 3.0 to 3.2 liters, with horsepower increasing from 172 to 200 on North American cars. The European version produced over 240 horsepower. Bottom: The interior of the 1984 Carrera, with all the controls within easy reach. Opposite page: The 911 Carrera 3.2 was available as a coupe, Targa, and cabriolet in 1984. The cabriolet was the first open Porsche without a roll bar since 1965.

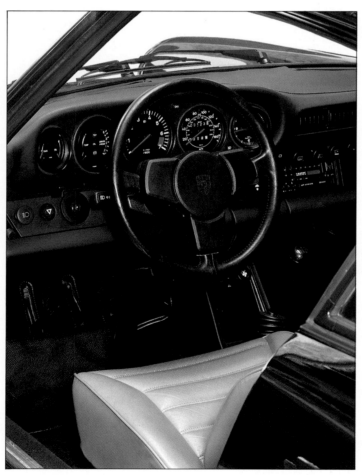

North America. The major option on the 911SC was the factory-installed 930 Turbo-style rear spoiler seen since 1978.

The year 1983 was the year of the 911SC cabriolet. This was the model that so many Porsche enthusiasts had been waiting for. The first design of the car was displayed on a 930 Turbo at the 1981 Frankfurt Auto Show. Orders were taken more than a year in advance. The first few hundred cars, available only in white or red, were spoken for before they reached the shores of North America. This was the first true convertible offered by the factory since 1965, when the 356C cabriolet went out of production. The new cabriolet was advertised as the world's fastest production convertible. The top had a steel panel between the fabric of the lining and the cloth top to keep the aerodynamically designed roof from puffing up at high speeds, and it featured a zip-out rear window. The engineers were able to retain the same 2 + 2 seating dimensions, with the same rear fold-up seats slightly shorter than those in the Targa and coupe, whether the top was up or down. The rear seating space was fine for kids, but the leg room was not spacious enough to be comfortable for an adult on any extended trip. Total sales for all models of Porsches for the year, including the 944 and 928, was 21,831. The two major markets were Europe and North America, with the United States receiving half of Porsche's worldwide production each year; half of the U.S. cars entered the California market.

Porsche made changes each year, whether it was a name change, an addition or deletion of a model, or even something as small as a change in paint colors. At the beginning of the 1984 model year, the 911SC was renamed the Carrera, a name reserved for Porsche's top products. The engine was increased from 3.0 to 3.2 liters, and the car could go from 0 to 60 mph (96.5 kph) in 6.2 seconds, with a top speed of 146 mph (234 kph).

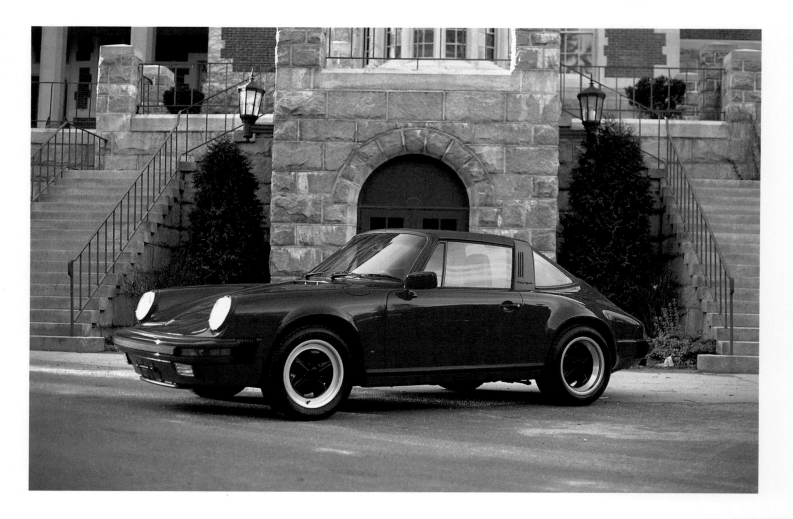

The most expensive option on the Carrera was a Turbo Look. This fancy body included the fender flares and the rear deck wing of the European Turbo, and everything else the Turbo had including the high performance brakes—the only thing missing was the turbo engine.

It should be pointed out that driving a rear-weighted configuration vehicle such as the 911 takes a little getting used to. Practice does help, especially if one is in the habit of entering exit ramps a bit too fast. If the driver is not prepared, the car can end up with some of its paint on the guardrail. The weight of the engine causes the car's tail to swing round during cornering if the driver lets up on the accelerator, creating quite an interesting feeling for the driver. Porsche continued to develop lighter exotic alloys to reduce the weight of the engine and transaxle.

The next year began a new era for Porsche. On September 1, 1984, the company's wholly owned subsidiary, Porsche Cars of North America, Inc., took over responsibility for all of the factory's marketing and service operations in the United States. Porsche decided not to renew its marketing agreement with Volkswagen of America, an agreement that had been in force since 1969. The new company would be headquartered in Reno, Nevada, where it is located today. Despite the U.S. change, Canadian dealerships continue to operate as Volkswagen Canada Inc.

Few changes were appearing on the 911 models in the mid-1980s besides a revision of the ventilation and heating system. Each year new colors were added and some were taken away. For an extra charge, the customer could always select the "paint to sample" option if the standard colors were not what he or she wanted. By 1986, Porsche started to make products that would have the same performance potential worldwide, made easier by the fact that Europe was instituting unleaded fuel regulations that forced manufacturers to offer catalytic-equipped cars.

After an absence of seven years, the decision was made to export the 911 Turbo, formerly called the 930 Turbo, to North America. The 930 never really left North America, since many individuals had imported the European cars through the "gray market" and then had them federalized, at a cost that far exceeded the new 1986 price. By the following year, the Turbo could be ordered in either a coupe or a convertible, and the Carrera, as always, had both options as well as the Targa as a third choice.

THE 959

It started in 1980, when Porsche announced that it would create a Porsche for the street that could match the performance of a race car. It is hard to determine when the 959 was first shown as a street car. Many of the 911 engineering advances of the 1980s were developments from the 959. In 1983, the 959 was on display as a racing Gruppe (Group) B race car at the Frankfurt Auto Show. The exterior skin was made out of Kevlar and aluminum, and by the following year, the design, incorporating the 911, was copied by after-market car shops all over California.

The competition version of the 959 was labeled 961, and a prototype raced at the Paris–Dakar rally (which it won in 1984). Customers were anxious to know when it would be a street car and whether it would be federalized to come to the United States and Canada. But the factory had no comment.

By 1987, this four-wheel-drive, six-speed transmission car was being driven on the roads in Europe. The top speed was said to be over 193 mph (311 kph), accelerating from 0 to 60 mph (96.5 kph) in 3.7 seconds, though there are not too many streets where one can go that fast. Even though the North American market was also

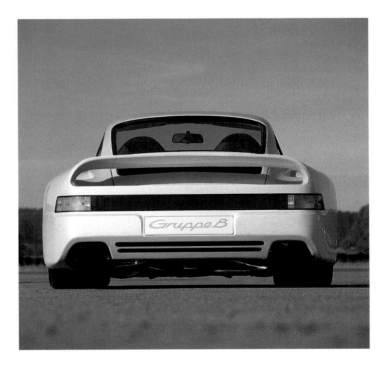

The rear of the fantastic and instantly successful 1983 Group B design study, which became the 959.

very interested in the 959, it was decided that the car could not meet the emissions and bumper-height regulations needed for federalization. It would have been too costly to make these changes for only the limited number that would have been produced for that market.

Anyone who has ever driven a 959 cannot say enough about it; they rave, and they get this far-off-look in their eyes, as if they have been somewhere out in the cosmos and have returned to tell about it.

THE 1990s

The full Porsche lineup for 1991 included the 944 coupe and cabriolet (discontinued worldwide for 1992 and replaced by the 968 six-speed [see page 100]), the 928S4 and 928GT, and a total of ten different combinations for the 911 model, including the top-of-the-line 911 Turbo.

Porsche stands for perfection. That sounds just like the company's advertising campaign, but anyone who looks at the new cars each year cannot doubt that these cars are outstanding. In the 1990s, the classic 911 became available in the Carrera 2 and the Carrera 4, the latter with fully automatic, "intelligent" all-wheel drive. Both models have the 6-cylinder engine and 247 horsepower at 6,100 rpm and can accelerate from 0 to 60 mph (96.5 kph) in 5.5 seconds. This 3.6-liter engine continues to be air-cooled with a top speed of 162 mph (261 kph). The only places to add water are the windshield and headlight washer reservoir.

The Carrera 2 and 4 could be called the ultimate driving machines. The body can be ordered in all three styles: coupe, Targa, and cabriolet. The rear features a spoiler that lays flat on the engine lid but extends automatically as higher speeds are reached for improved handling and additional engine cooling. It also retracts below 10 mph (16 kph). The Porsche owner's manual states that "if the spoiler does not extend at speeds above 80 kph (50 mph), a warning light will appear in

"Turbo"). In 1976, the rear spoiler was made larger, with two air intakes so that more air could be transferred to the engine and air-conditioner. When the wider wheels and tires were added, the front wheel openings were flared.

The initial North American engine possessed thermal reactors and an air pump to meet the emissions laws. This caused a decrease in the horsepower compared to the European engines—245 vs. 260 horsepower at 5,500 rpm. (By 1979, all turbos had air pumps.) There was a visual difference between a North American 930 and those for all other markets. The North American version did not have the rear fog lamp mounted under the left side bumper extension, the rear reflectors in the rubber bumper strips, or the two small rectangular lights just ahead of the doors (which were directionals only).

In 1977, for the 1978 model year, Porsche increased the car's power to an unbelievable 300 horsepower (265 for North America). The Turbo could now go from 0 to 60 mph (96.5 kph) in 5.3 seconds. The brakes were improved for quicker stopping and now had the cross-ventilated discs with the four-piston calipers from the racing 917, as seen on the 1974 Turbo prototypes. The external difference between the early Turbos and the later models was the redesigned rear spoiler with one intake area with louvers facing forward and a high rubber edge.

The last of the North American 930 Turbos were delivered by the end of the 1979 model year, after emissions laws became too strict for this car to meet the requirements. It was still produced for the European market, and many Porsche enthusiasts purchased the cars through Europe and had them federalized to U.S. and Canadian specifications at a very dear price.

By 1986, the Turbo was back in North America as part of the Porsche lineup. Now called the 911 Turbo, it was available worldwide, meeting every country's regulations.

A new body style was an option for the 911 Turbo in 1987, which had the appearance of the 935 race car. The new look, called the 930S, included a sloping nose with retract-able headlights. There were air scoops in front of the rear wheels to help cool the engine and brakes and small functional air vent slits behind the headlights. This body style could also be ordered on the coupe, Targa, or cabriolet.

For the 1990s, a new Turbo was on the drawing boards. For the 1992 model year, more than seventeen years after the earliest turbocharged production car, top track speed was 168 mph (270 kph) with acceleration of 0 to 60 mph (96.5 kph) in 4.8 seconds. The 3.3-liter, 6-cylinder, water-cooled, horizontally opposed turbocharged engine was rated at 315 horsepower at 5,750 rpm. Much was improved, including the new exhaust system, a larger air-to-air inter-cooler, and an electronic ignition system now fully computerized to minimize emissions and increase power.

In addition, the body was redesigned, with contoured bumpers front and rear and the new aerodynamic front and rear spoiler. The side-view mirrors on each door were also changed in shape. The 17-inch lightweight alloy wheels were now 7 inches wide in front and 9 inches wide at the rear. The underside included suspension changes and upgrades from engineering experience on the race cars. In addition, the five-speed transmission was revised with sportier gear ratios.

There isn't much more to ask for on this 911 Turbo. Standard equipment includes air bags for both the driver and passenger, antilock braking system, ZR-rated steel-belted radial tires, air-conditioning with automatic climate control, and tinted windows. The leather bucket seats recline and have electric height adjustments, and the radio includes an AM/FM digital stereo and cassette with eight speakers. There are also power windows, an electric sunroof, heated windshield-washer nozzles, heated outside mirrors, and an alarm system that shows that it is engaged by a blinking light on the top of the door lock buttons. The only options available are special metallic paint, limited-slip differential, a compact disc player, heated front seats, an electrically controlled lumbar support seat, sports seats, and the gathered-leather seat upholstery.

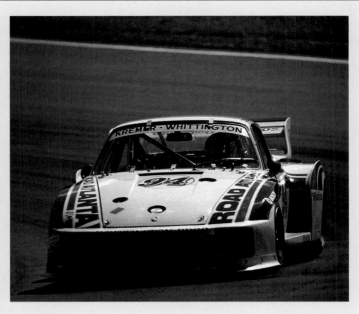

Top right: *The Team Whittington 935 at the Watkins Glen 6-hour race in 1979.* Bottom: *In 1987, Porsche offered a new body-style option for the 911 Turbo that copied its styling from the successful Porsche 935 race car.* Top left: *Detail photograph of the air scoops that assisted in bringing air to the engine and brakes for cooling.*

Right: *The 1992 America Roadster. Opposite page: A 1952 Porsche America Roadster. Only eleven of these cars are known to remain. This well-preserved car still has its original tires and muffler. The body was made by Gläser; their badge, affixed to the side of the car, is shown in the upper left-hand corner.*

Porsche 911 America Roadster

In 1952, Porsche introduced a car for the U.S. market called the America Roadster (see page 24). It was designed to be used as a street car, but by removing a few heavy items, the car became very competitive in Sports Car Club of America (SCCA) racing events.

For 1992, the fortieth anniversary of Porsche's first road racing victories in the United States, a new America Roadster was introduced—this time as a 911, available only as a cabriolet. Its body has the wide front and rear flared fenders similar to the 1992 911 Turbo, with the new aerodynamic side-view mirror design. The wheels are also from the Turbo: 7×7 inches in front and 9×17 inches at the rear, with the new five-spoke design. The engine is the 3.6-liter, normally aspirated 6-cylinder from the Carrera, with 247 horsepower at 6,100 rpm; the transmission choices are the five-speed manual or the Tiptronic dual function. The best part is that the brakes and suspension are from the 911 Turbo with independent coil springs at the front and rear. There is a very good chance that the Porsche 911 America Roadster will become a collectible, as the factory has made the decision to limit the number produced to 250 for the 1992 model year. No Porsche convertibles in the United States will have back seats because of the safety regulations mandating rear-seat shoulder belts.

gravel guards at the rear, and front and rear spoilers. The first Turbos that came to North America had a very unusual black and white checkered flag fabric on the seat inserts and door panels. This same pattern was also seen on early 928s, but fortunately for the buying public, it did not last very long.

The horsepower on the 924 Turbo was 170 at 5,500 rpm in the European market and 143 at 5,500 rpm in the North American market. The 924 Turbo weighed 60 pounds (27 kg) more than the 924, requiring adjustments including stiffer shocks, heavier antiroll bars, and recalibrated front springs due to its increased performance. Porsche continued to add extras each year, including rear seat belts, extra soundproofing, suspension improvements, and halogen headlights. In 1981, the Turbo was modified and four-wheel disc brakes became standard on both the 924 and 924 Turbo. The 924s were never quite respected as a Porsche in the North American market, but that same market was ready for the 924 Turbo they had heard about in all the automotive magazines. The Turbo was discontinued in the summer of 1982, except for a small number for the Italian market.

Other variations of the 924 included: in 1979, a Carrera GT for racing (only four hundred were made to satisfy Group 4 homologation requirements of FISA [Federation Internationale Sportif Automobile]); in 1980, a 924 D (a special kit for SCCA ''D Production''); also in 1980, a 924 Carrera Le Mans GT ''P'' (specially built prototypes for the 1980 Le Mans race with 917 brakes); a Carrera GTS for Group 4 competition; a Rally Package with higher ground clearance, heavy-duty suspension, and an antiroll bar; and, in 1981, the Carrera GTS for Group 4 and Trans-Am racing.

At the Frankfurt Auto Show in September 1981, an all-new Porsche was introduced: the 944. During this time, the 924 and 924 Turbo were taken off the market in North America, but they continued to be produced for

Europe and the United Kingdom with an updated interior. In February 1982, the 100,000th 924 came off the production line.

In 1986, for the 1987 model year, the 924 was upgraded for all markets, and a new 924S was introduced as the latest entry-level Porsche. This new car was built with 944 brakes, electrical system, suspension, and drivetrain. The engine was also straight from the 944, but in the lighter 924 body. The car possessed air-conditioning, tinted glass, heated power-remote mirrors, power steering, power windows, and a power antenna as standard equipment. The new S was as fast as the 944 Turbo when flat out and could rival the Turbo in acceleration. A bargain Porsche, optional equipment for it included a radio/tape player, limited-slip differential, automatic transmission, electric sunroof, and a rear window wiper. Porsche chose to discontinue this car at the end of 1988.

Opposite page: A 1981 924 Carrera GTS. When introduced, this was the fastest 4-cylinder road car in the world. Although not allowed on public roads in North America, it was street legal in Germany. Above: A 1980 Porsche Turbo "Le Mans," a prototype specially built for the Le Mans 24-Hour endurance race. It used the brakes

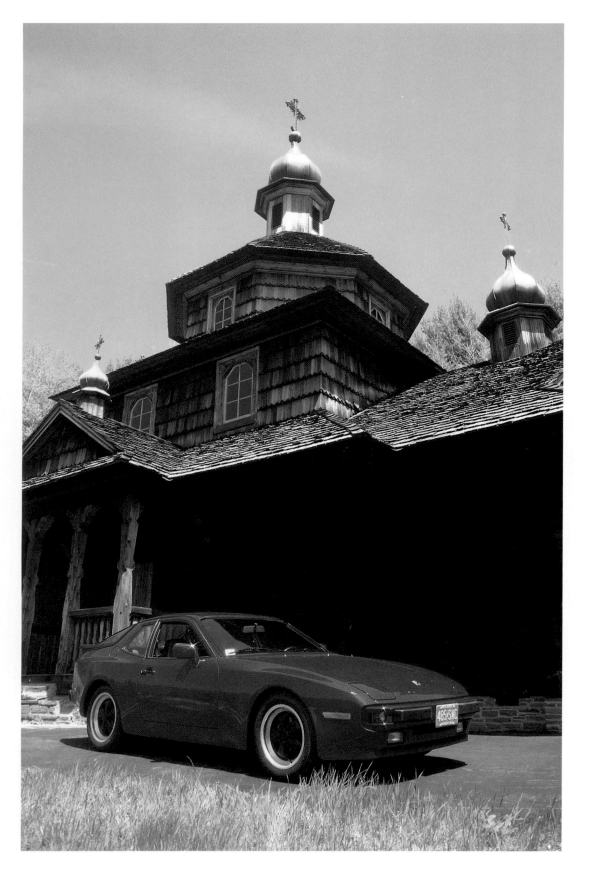

THE 944, 944S, AND 944 TURBO

Although the arrival of the 944 was announced in 1981 in Europe, it was not officially introduced to the North American market until May 1982 as a 1983 model. The U.S. dealers received so many advance orders that there was a six-month waiting list for delivery. The reason for all the delays was that the engine had not been fully tested: Porsche wanted to be sure this engine was a true Porsche product. Porsche had to please the buying public and especially wanted the automotive press to give the car high marks.

The 944 had a 2.5-liter engine by Porsche, revised bodywork, and a great price. The standard options available on this model were the same as other models.

It was said that the 944's engine was half of the 928 V–8, but this was never true. However, the technology gained from the 928 power plant was transferred to the development of this new 4-cylinder. The European horsepower was 160 at 5,800 rpm and the North American cars had 143 horsepower at 5,500 rpm. To keep the noise level down, which had been a problem with the 924, the engineers used a special balance-shaft design that they paid Mitsubishi a patent fee to use. Porsche also worked on other factors to quiet the ride and succeeded.

The chassis and body shell of the 944 were from the 924, but the fenders were flared (resembling the 924 Carrera GT race car) for the wider tires and wheels. A front air dam was added and a rear spoiler attached to the bottom of the hatchback window. As with the 924, the steering wheel still did not leave adequate clearance between the driver's hands and legs when in a turn. This problem was later addressed by lowering the seats, raising the steering wheel, and offering a smaller steering wheel as an option. This car was finally a Porsche's Porsche. It was everything that the 924 should have been.

In 1985, the interior of the 944 was completely changed, with a new dash design and a rearranged instrument panel for better viewing. The factory figures state that the 944 could go from 0 to 60 (96.5 kph) in 8.3 seconds with a top speed of 130 mph (109 kph). The 924 Turbo would reach 0 to 60 mph (96.5 kph) in 9.1 seconds. Now how fast could a 944 Turbo fly?

At a top speed of over 150 mph (241 kph) with 217 horsepower at 5,800 rpm, the 944 Turbo, introduced at the end of 1985, was definitely a fast runner. It had excellent high-end range and could go from 0 to 60 mph (96.5 kph) in 6.1 seconds. The Turbo's outer skin differed from that of the normally aspirated model, with a revised nose with wide slots for cooling and a rear underbody pan for better high-speed stability. A front and rear spoiler and wider wheels and tires were included. The wheels that

were used had the five-hole design, sometimes called "phone dial" wheels, copied from the early 928s.

In Germany in 1986, the Porsche 944 Turbo Cup racing series was introduced, featuring near-standard models with catalytic converters and 220 horsepower (increased to 250 horsepower by the following year). A new "sports" suspension kit became available as an option for street cars following the Turbo Cup racing developments. The factory announced in 1987, for the 1988 model year, a special edition of 1,000 models of the Turbo S to be produced to similar specifications as the Turbo Cup series cars.

By mid-1986, a newer 944 was announced: the 944S. The major change was the engine; it now had twin-cams and four valves per cylinder, similar to the 928S in technology, but with no interchangeable parts. The horsepower was now raised to 188 at 6,000 rpm and the top speed was over 140 mph (225 kph). By 1987, both the 944 Turbo and the 944S now had ABS (antilock braking system) as an option (standard on all models in 1989). Air bags were standard on the Turbo for both the driver and the passenger and were optional on the 944 and 944S. Porsche was the first automotive manufacturer that offered air bags for the passenger, optional or standard.

Porsche added more standard equipment to the cars each year, and by 1988, this included air-conditioning, power windows and locks, a rear spoiler, electric height adjustment for the driver's seat, heated rear window, and an indicator that sensed the brake-pad wear.

Porsche always added limited edition models to its lines. These cars were made with special treatment, and they also had special features. One such special edition car was called a 944 TurboS, only 700 of which were built in 1988. The engine had 30 more horsepower than the regular Turbo and went from 0 to 60 mph (96.5 km) in 5.5 seconds, with a top speed of 162 mph (261 kph). The

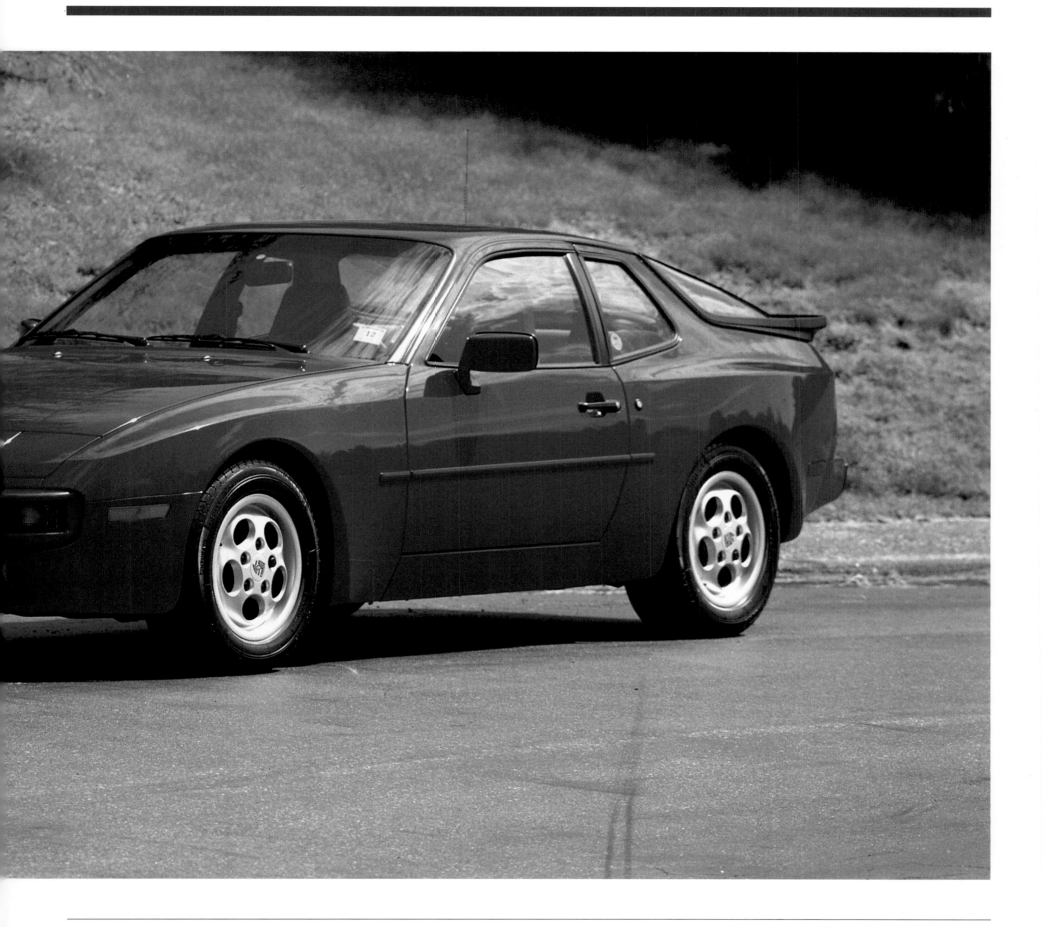

suspension was designed with stiffer springs, the shock absorbers were firmer, and the antiroll bars were heavier in order to control this higher-performance street car.

There were a lot of Porsches to pick from, in a wide range of prices, in 1989. The 944S was replaced by the 944S2, with a new 3.0-liter engine now up to 208 horsepower. A new 944 S2 cabriolet, the car Porsche enthusiasts had been awaiting for over three years, was ready for delivery. There were also more standard equipment items, including cruise control, a removable electric sun-

roof, and an alarm system that blinked a light in the top of the door lock when engaged. The least expensive car in the line was the 944.

The 944, 944S2, and 944 Turbo were all available in 1989. By 1990 there was only the 944S2 in a coupe or cabriolet. In 1989, the last year that the 944 Turbo was produced, the turbocharger was increased in size and the horsepower was up to 247 at 6,000 rpm. The new car that replaces the 944 is the 968 for the 1992 model year, a car said to be close to the 911 Carrera 2 (see page 100).

A 1991 944 S2.

Special Editions

Every so often, to keep the attention of the Porsche buyer, the factory will introduce a special edition Porsche that has some extra features over the basic line and that is limited in the number produced. The changes offered on these specials and their limited production adds to the rarity of the model and helps to hold the model's value.

The 911SC Weissach Coupe

Only 400 of the exclusive limited edition 911SC Weissach Coupes were made. They were almost sold out before they reached the North American shores. The car was basically a 1980 SC with all the standard features: a flat-6, horizontally opposed, 3.0-liter engine, 172 horsepower at 5,500 rpm. It could reach 0 to 60 mph (96.5 kph) in 6.5 seconds in second gear, with a top speed of 140 mph (225 kph). The added goodies included a functional spoiler under the nose and a "whale tail" spoiler at the rear (last seen on the 911 Turbo). During high-speed driving, these spoilers stabilized the car; they also made it look fast in traffic.

The other additions included sports shocks and special Pirelli CN36 tires. There were special sealed-beam halogen headlights (the U.S. regulations at the time required sealed beams), an electric antenna, rear speakers (the radio was extra), and electrically heated mirrors on both sides (only one was standard).

These cars were available in only two colors: black or champagne gold. The wheels were forged alloy with platinum metallic centers with the Porsche crest. The interior was light beige leather with contrasting burgundy piping on the seats, and the floor had plush burgundy carpeting—a very attractive combination.

Lower left: The rugged Porsche forged-aluminum alloy wheels were standard equipment on the 911SC Weissach Coupes. First introduced on the new 1967 911S, they steadily grew in width to accommodate improvements in suspension and tire technology. Lower right: In 1980, the center console, the three-spoke, 15-inch (38-cm) steering wheel, and electric windows all became standard on the 911 models. Seen here is the Weissach Coupe's light beige leather interior with contrasting burgundy piping.

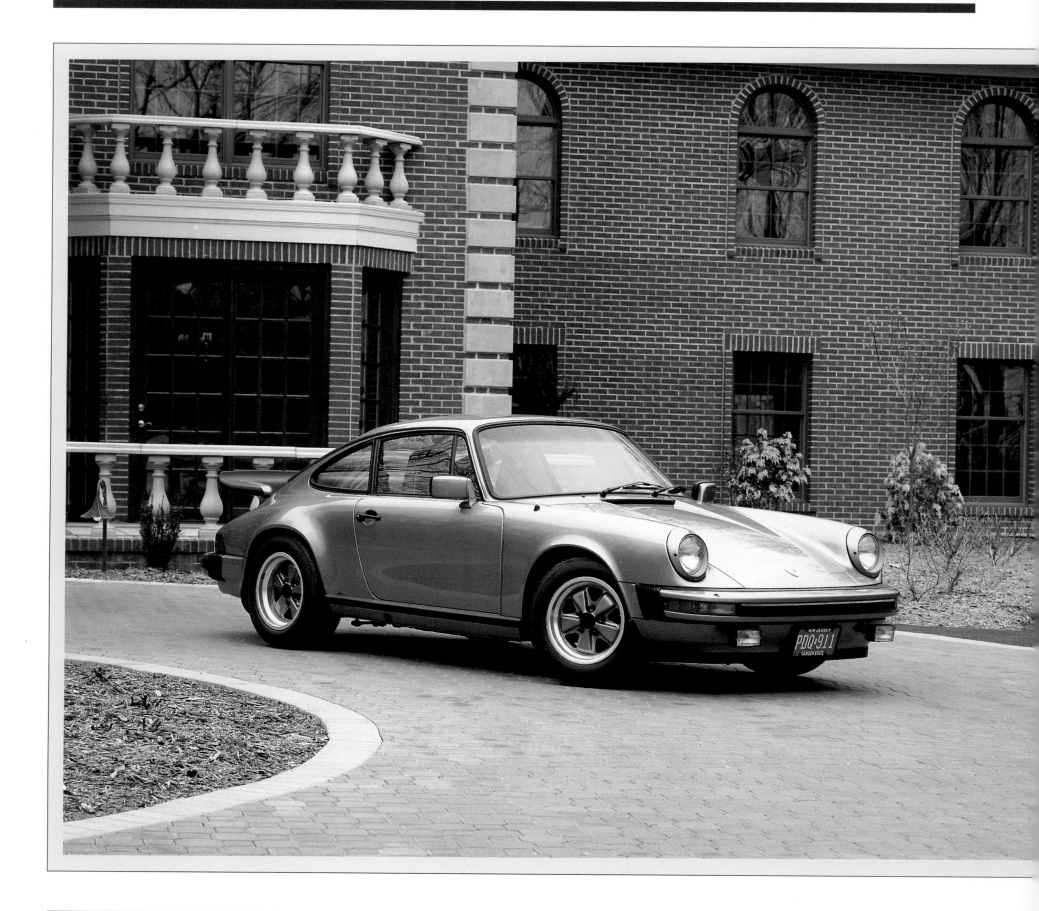

The Martini, the Sebring '79, and the Le Mans

A Martini Edition 924 was produced for sale in the spring of 1977, celebrating two world championship crowns earned by Porsche the year before in Group 5 and Group 6 racing. All the cars were painted white with the Martini stripes on both sides. The interior included deep red pile carpets and trim changes.

The Sebring '79 was produced for the U.S. market, with a total of 1,300 cars painted bright orange-red. The script lettering "Sebring 79" was written in white on the front fender, under the black, white, and gold striping on the side, like the pace car at the famous 12-Hours of Sebring (Florida) race.

A Le Mans edition was introduced later for the European market, honoring the three 1980 finishes by Porsche 924 Carrera GTRs (sixth, twelfth, and thirteenth) at the famous 24-hour race in France. These cars were painted white, with gold, red, and black striping on the side. The word "Le Mans" was lettered on the front fender. As many as one hundred of these special edition Porsches were sent to England, and only a few reached the Australian shores because of the quota system in place there.

The 924 Weissach

The 924 Weissach special edition was designed for the purpose of encouraging the sale of more cars. This model was available only in metallic platinum, which looked close to a metallic light brown. Only a limited number were produced for the North American market in 1981. Featuring special wheels and the rear spoiler from the Turbo, it was a very strong-looking car.

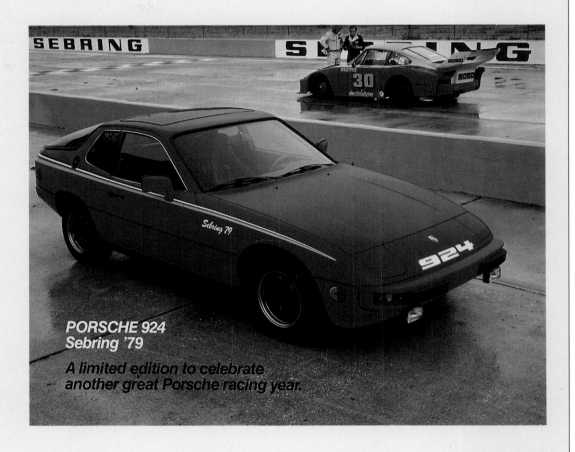

PORSCHE 924
Sebring '79

A limited edition to celebrate another great Porsche racing year.

The 928 Weissach Special Edition

This special model 928 followed in the tradition of other Weissach specials, with a limited production of only 205 cars. Mechanically, everything was the same. The difference was in the champagne gold metallic paint scheme with the matching brushed gold-colored alloy wheels—a beautiful combination. A spoiler was added to the rear hatchback window and another to the lower front of the nose. The interior included an electric sunroof, a digital radio, and special two-toned leather throughout. The best addition was the three-piece Porsche luggage set that was made from the same leather as the interior If you happen to get the chance to buy one of these special edition 928s, I wonder if the luggage will still be part of the deal!

Opposite page: The 911SC Weissach Coupe offered as a special edition in 1980. Above: To commemorate their victories at Sebring in 1979, Porsche offered a special limited edition "Sebring '79" 924 in the United States market.

THE 928

Originally called Project 928, the Porsche 928 was introduced at the Geneva Automobile Salon in March 1977. The original idea for the 928 took place during the early 1970s, when the people at Porsche were thinking about a possible successor to the famous 911. It had been a concern for many years that the 911 buyer might just suddenly stop buying; with more than half of its production coming to the United States, Porsche had to seriously consider that market. But it is also quite possible that the development of the new 928 had nothing to do with replacing the 911, and that the factory wanted to prove that it could build a car with a water-cooled engine that was in front, rather than air-cooled and mounted in the rear.

The engineers knew that a new car from Porsche had to be new from the ground up, and that was how the project worked from beginning to end. Every part was designed from scratch. About halfway through the project the world had an energy crisis, which quickly changed some of the thinking at Porsche. But the project continued with better ideas for a more energy-conscious buyer. Since the car was created from the drawing board, it did not have to resemble any other Porsche, and the new car definitely looked different. We are now used to the design, but in 1977, many thought of it as strange, unusual, futuristic, even spaceship-looking. But, the question at the time was: would the traditional Porsche fan have interest in this new front-engined, water-cooled car? As it turned out, a new kind of Porsche buyer purchased this trendy car. In 1992, the 928 S4 (four-speed automatic) and GT (five-speed manual transmission) were offered. The 928 GTS is the newest model in this line.

When the new 928 was first driven by the motor press of the world, it received many outstanding awards. They called it the new breed of supercar.

THE DEVELOPMENT

Starting from scratch was the best challenge: the ideas were limitless, but the demands heavy. The new car had to be able to accommodate future regulations, and it had to stand the test of time, as the 356 and 911 had. The 356 series had continued for fifteen years. By 1977, the year of the 928's introduction, the 911 was already in its thirteenth year, with no end in sight.

The original idea for the 928 was on the drawing boards by 1971, and after a frantic race for time, a completed skeleton model was ready by 1972, followed by the unveiling of a full-scale model in the fall of the next year.

The first change from other Porsches was the engine. A 6-cylinder was considered, but it was decided that the engine definitely had to be performance-oriented, keeping with the company's image, and there had to be room for expansion. Another major requirement was the ability to meet future legislation for emissions. The final decision was a water-cooled 90-degree V–8.

Top: A 1978 Porsche 928. The most advanced feature was the Weissach rear axle, which automatically adjusted to the driver's input, thus creating great confidence in the car's handling abilities. Lower left: A 928 receives its paint in a special ventilated paint booth. The painter removed his mask for this photograph. Bottom right: A worker begins to install the driver's seat track in a 928. The extra-large transmission hump identifies this as an automatic model, which requires different rear seats than the smaller five-speed manual model.

Deciding where to build the car was the next problem. The factory at Stuttgart-Zuffenhausen, where over 13,000 911s were being produced, estimated that 5,000 928s could be produced. They switched some of the 911 production over to 928. The total capacity was 20,000 a year.

THE LOOK, THE FEEL, THE IMAGE, THE 928

Look at the bumpers—the car looks like it has none. This is because the design engineers integrated the polyurethane-paneled bumpers into the body and carefully painted the body and bumpers to match. To keep the car from getting overweight, the V–8 engine, doors, front hood, and fenders were made of aluminum. Porsche had to find new paint adhesions for the steel, aluminum, and polyurethane, for all had to look equal in color and be long-lasting.

The headlights of the 928 are set into the body, raised by an electric motor. The North American version has both high and low beams in one set of lights. In Europe the pop-up lights are only for the low beams, and the high-beam lights are set into the front bumper; on those cars, the headlight height adjustment can be changed with a knob on the floor next to the driver's thigh.

When sitting in the driver's seat, you get the feeling you can actually fly. The instrument panel has the appearance of the interior of an airplane. The whole instrument cluster moves up and down along with the steering wheel so the driver can see all the dials all the time. Even the pedal positions are adjustable. The electrically adjustable outside mirrors are heated for humid or icy days and nights. The secure design of the interior puts the driver and passengers in a safety cocoon. The rear seating (2 + 2), does not have enough room for an adult on a cross-country trip but is adequate for young children or short rides when the front seats are in the mid-position. The back seats also fold down separately to add more space in the hatchback trunk area.

The handling is definitely quick; the 50–50 weight distribution was accomplished by mounting the engine in the front, with the combined gearbox and final drive assembly in the rear. The famous Weissach rear axle,

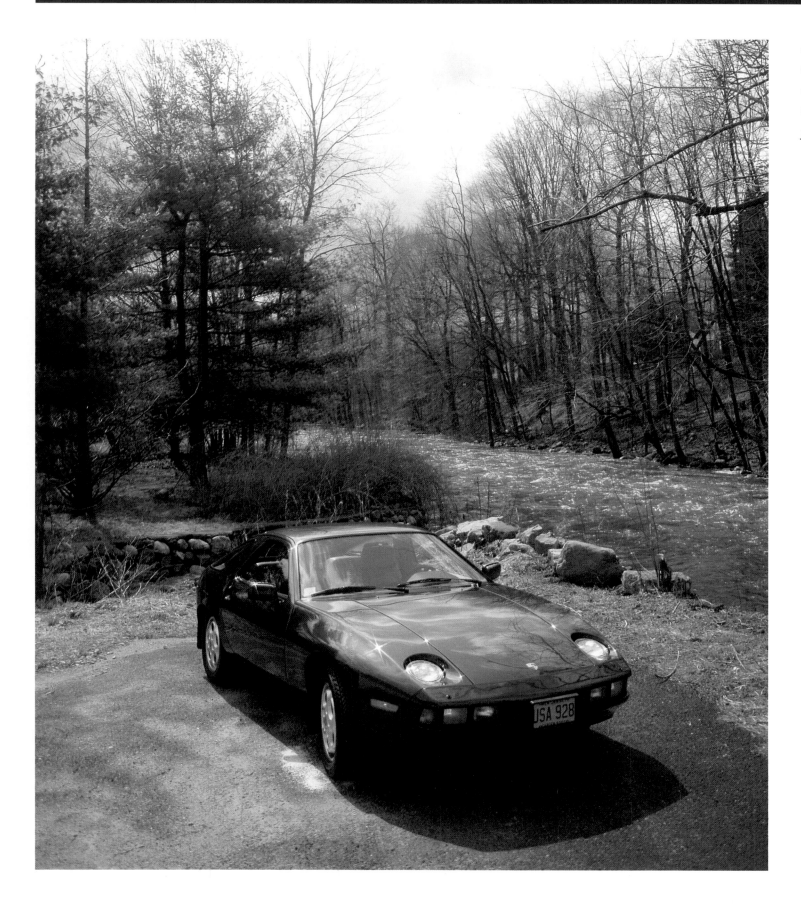

A 1980 Porsche 928. The optional climate control and sunroof were the two most important changes from 1979.

CHAPTER SIX

WHAT IS NEW FROM PORSCHE?

THE 968

The latest from Porsche in 1992 is the 968. This newest of cars from Stuttgart-Zuffenhausen, the 911 and 928 Porsche factory, is derived from the 911, the 928, and the 959, but it replaces the ten-year-old 944.

Porsche says the 968 is 80 percent a newly designed car. The transmission is a six-speed manual gearbox; the sixth gear is slightly longer than the fifth used to be, so it still has a lot of torque for pulling away from traffic. Both fifth and sixth are overdrive gears. Able to be revved up to red-line one extra time when shifting, this new six-speed manual transmission should even be more fun to drive. But every Porsche is fun to drive, whether it has an automatic, four-, five-, or now six-speed transmission. For the automatic, Porsche is using a four-speed Tiptronic revised from the transmission used on the Carrera 2. Now all automatic-transmissioned cars coming into North America will have a shiftlock, so drivers cannot take out the ignition key unless the shift lever is in park. Another safety feature will not let the driver move the shift lever out of park unless the brake pedal is depressed.

If you look at the 968 from the front, you can see some of the 911 lines above the hood. The pop-up headlights and front fenders raised into the hoodline look like they were taken from the 928, with a little 959 angling thrown in. The roofline is from the 944, as is the rear glass. The doors have that 944 look, and the fog lights integrated in the bumpers resemble the 928 after a diet. The interior door panels appear to be taken from the 911.

Porsche was never one for wasting leftover parts from the last model. They used the 356 engines in the early 912s and the 914 2.0-liter engines in the 912Es. Even the door handles from the early 911s showed up on the next model until they were used up.

Porsche also has something new happening all the time. This new baby looks just like its older relatives. But

Little-Known Information

In North America, expensive automobile manufacturers have been hurt by the terrible recession, as well as the new luxury tax in the United States added onto cars priced over $20,000. One of the hardest hit was Porsche, which dropped over 50 percent of its sales in North America from 1990 to 1991. Porsche hopes to gain back some of its lost customers with the new 968. The company continues to remain profitable even though it builds far fewer cars than most other automobile manufacturers. Porsche will build 5,000 to 6,000 of the new 968s the first year. About 1,500 of these cars will come to North America (only 25 percent of production compared to 50 percent in years past). The cars are individually manufactured to your specifications, and you can even go to Germany to pick up what you ordered. I wonder if you could do that in Japan?

the horsepower has changed from 208 at 5,800 rpm on the 944 to 236 at 6,200 rpm on the 968. The torque has been increased from 207 to 225 foot-pounds at 4,100 rpm, the highest for any normally aspirated 3.0-liter engine no matter how many cylinders in the engine. This engine still has only four cylinders.

After using the same chassis from the 944 Turbo, Porsche revised the springs, shocks, and antiroll bars. If the customer prefers a harder ride and more rubber on the road, a special handling package can be ordered as an option. This sports suspension package includes 17-inch aluminum wheels with wider front and rear tires (front 205/55ZR × 16 up to 225/45ZR × 17 and rear 225/50ZR × 16 up to 255/40ZR × 17). The suspension includes

Porsche's latest model, the 1992 968, available as a coupe or cabriolet.

stiffer springs, adjustable shock absorbers, larger brakes, and a device that adjusts the ride height.

The view from the rear of the car shows ''968'' in raised numbers above the embossed PORSCHE lettering. The bumpers are integrated into the body to give a beautiful uninterrupted flow. The light alloy wheels are the new five-spokes that were seen before on the 911 Turbo, and the aerodynamic side-view mirrors (also from the 911 Turbo) appear on all models.

Highlights from the 968 interior include the 944 dash, with a few gauges changed around. The clock has been moved to the center of the console; a digital temperature read-out takes up the old clock position. The top track speed is 156 mph (251 kph), compared to 149 mph (240 kph) for the 944. However, the speedometer reads up to 180 mph (288 kph), perhaps to accommodate future advances in engine design. According to the manufacturer's data, the acceleration is from 0 to 60 mph (96.5 kph) in 6.1 seconds with the manual transmission and 7.5 seconds with Tiptronic.

Because the 968 is built in Zuffenhausen, special orders can be easily handled; paint can even be swatched. Just pick out your best color, maybe from your favorite tie; Porsche will match it and paint your car to order.

One of the fun options is the remote CD player. You put the discs in the trunk-mounted system, select your plays from your seat, and listen from ten speakers hidden throughout the interior.

The 1992 911 line-up. A Carrera 2 cabriolet (top), a 911 Turbo (middle), and a Carrera 4 (bottom). The Carrera 4 was Porsche's first four-wheel-drive passenger car to be offered worldwide. Visually similar to the previous 911 models, it has a new and quite different chassis.

The 968 is available in 1992 in the coupe (with a rear spoiler) and the cabriolet—two very attractive options. The convertibles coming to North America have no back-seats because of the safety regulations mandating rear-seat shoulder belts, but the European model has the small seats like the 944 cabriolet. Backseat or no backseat, my choice still would be the convertible, especially with the new power-assisted and easy-to-operate top. The old design from the early Targa roof was finally updated.

When adding it all up, the new 968 is quicker, stops in less time, has greater handling, and is a better all-around Porsche than the 944. If you had put in your order when this book was written, you may have one already.

The Standard Models for the Early 1990s

The new cars for 1992 are the 968 and the America Roadster (see page 64), but the rest of the lineup is exciting too. The Porsche 911 is available in the Carrera 2 and Carrera 4; both cars can be ordered as a coupe, Targa, or cabriolet. The Carreras have the new five-spoke wheels from the 911 Turbo, and the side-view mirrors have been replaced with the new aerodynamic design. The 911 continues to be available as a Turbo. In addition, the 928 S4 (automatic) and 928 GT (five-speed manual transmission) look essentially the same, but the name designation on the back of the car will only say 928. The 1993 928 GTS will have a few styling changes to the fenders and the horse-power will be increased, with a top track speed of 171 mph (274 kph). In addition to the 1992 911 offerings, the 911 RS America is a new model that will also be available in 1993 (see opposite page for more information). Porsche always has something new to add to its lineup each year, and it is always worth waiting for.

The latest special edition from Porsche is the 1993 Porsche 911 RS America. A lighter version of the Carrera 2 by about 180 pounds (81 kg) and devoid of many accessories, it is meant for the serious driver.

The 1993 911 RS America

The latest news from Porsche for the 1993 model year is the 911 RS America. The "RS" designation (German for *Rennsport,* or "Race Sport") is traditionally reserved for the highest-performance Porsches. This new version Porsche is designed to handle more like a competition 911. It offers stiffer springs and shock absorbers, larger wheels and tires, and a larger-diameter front stabilizer bar than the normal 911 Carrera 2. It will be built in limited quantities for the North American market only, available in four colors: red, black, metallic silver, and metallic midnight blue.

To save on weight, the air conditioning systems, power steering, sunroof, and rear seats have been eliminated. The armrest/storage compartments have been replaced with "RS-style" door panels and simple door pull straps. The sound-deadening materials were also removed from the firewall and rear quarter panels. The retractable rear spoiler, motor and mechanism, was replaced with a large, lightweight fixed tail spoiler.

The RS America is equipped with skid-resistant, black brushed corduroy, form-fitting sports seats, which will enable you to keep in place when accelerating from 0 to 60 mph (96.5 kph) in just 5.4 seconds to a top track speed of 170 mph (272 kph). It is possible to order limited slip-differential, sunroof, air conditioning, and a stereo cassette radio as optional equipment on this model.

The RS America is not for everyone. The Porsche sales brochure states it all: "The RS never fails to deliver an aggressive, invigorating driving experience where the balance of power and nimble agility puts the driver in control of its unbridled spirit."

CHAPTER SEVEN

PORSCHE RACING

Page 104: *This 962 (chassis no. 962 106) was driven by Jim Busby and Darren Brassfield at the Laguna Seca, California, race in 1986. After racing in the 1987 season, this car was sold to a collector. Page 105: The 1989 Porsche Indy car. The steering wheel must be removed for the driver to enter or exit the car.*

went to a bullfight a few years ago in Spain. I sat in the front row and could see into the eyes of the bullfighter, not to mention the eyes of the bull. But it was the eyes of the bullfighter that most intrigued me.

I have been to many automobile races and have photographed the drivers from the pit area and track, shooting right into the cockpit, looking right into their faces. It fascinated me to see that the eyes of the bullfighter were the same as those of the race car drivers.

Does that mean anything? It could be that both are the type of person who enjoys getting close to the danger and excitement. They know their limits and love every minute of what they are doing and wouldn't change it for the world.

EARLY RACING
550/550A, RSK, RS60/RS61

The racing cars that Porsche develops are designed to sell cars. The factory spends money to make money. Many of the successful advanced developments made through the years for the track automobiles turned up on the street models the following year. Racing provided a quick way for the technical department to test an idea after it passed the safety development. Porsche always believed that racing was the only true test of a car's value. One twenty-four-hour race was as good a test as two to three years in the hands of an average driver on the street.

In the early 1950s, when the Porsche was first manufactured and exported to North America, the "gentleman racer" considered the car for road racing. The 356 was first thought of as a good rally vehicle and later was taken to track events, where it easily beat the MGs and Simcas in the small bore class (under 1,500cc). In Europe,

however, where racing was taken more seriously, it was a different matter. High-performance small sports racers flew by the Porsches in sprint events and the only saving grace was a long-distance race. Porsche won rallies in 1950 with the 1.1-liter 356.

That same year, Walter Glöckler produced a sports-racing car with Porsche components, a 1.1-liter Porsche engine, and VW running gear. It was a single-seater open car with the driver placed almost in the center, similar to past designs of early race cars that Porsche had been involved with, such as the Cisitalia. That first year, the car won the under-1,100cc sports-car class in Germany.

Starting in 1951, Porsche made an agreement with Glöckler to produce a sports-racing car using the Porsche name in exchange for the use of the latest in engine technology. The cars became known as the Glöckler-Porsches. Changes were made on each car built, such as increasing the size of the interior and adding headlights—one even had a removable roof. This was the beginning of a history of winning races within Europe and, by late 1951, in North America as well. This racer—now with a 1.5-liter engine and weighing only 990 pounds (446 kg)—broke many records, from short sprints to long-distance endurance events. The name "Porsche" was now recorded and mentioned in newspapers, which was the free advertising that Porsche needed.

In 1951 and 1952, Porsche's aluminum-bodied coupes with the 1.1-liter engine (1,100cc) won their class at the 24-hour race at Le Mans, France. By 1952, a lightweight America Roadster was offered to the North American racer through the New York importer Max Hoffman with delivery for the following year (see page 24). Other than this small effort, Porsche did not feel ready to produce a true race car for its buyers. The following year, the English-language sales brochures (printed in Germany) listed the 1952 racing results from Italy, France, Holland, Austria, Germany, Portugal, Sweden, and the United States.

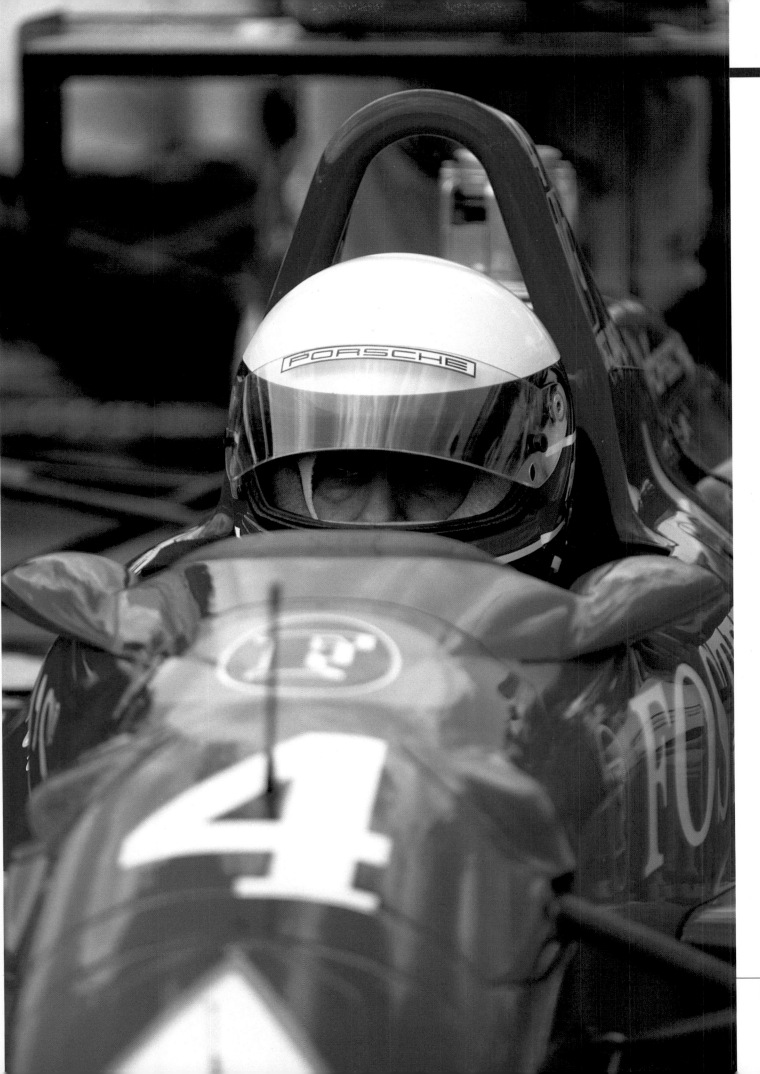

Top left: Porsche had a special poster made to announce its victories in the 1953 Carrera Panamericana. José Herrarte drove the second Porsche Spyder ever built to a class win in this race, which took a week and went from the Guatemalan to the U.S. borders. Top right: In the mid-1950s, Porsche produced a sales flier to advertise the Type 550 Spyder race cars.

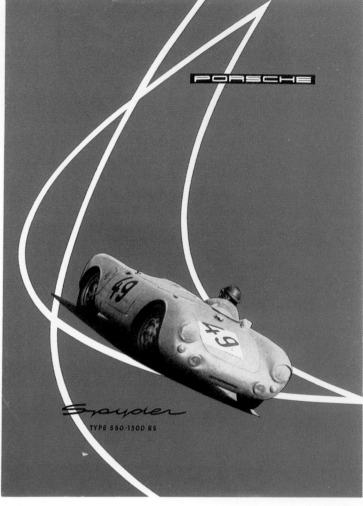

Besides winning the Italian Championship for 1,500cc Gran Turismo, Porsche had also won the German Championship in both the 1,100cc and 1,500cc categories, as well as other first, second, and third place wins. These events were not won by race cars, but with street cars prepared for track events. In many cases, the cars were actually driven to and from the event and not trailered.

Two Type 550 Porsches were commissioned to be built by Glöckler for 1953. Both cars (serial numbers 550-01 and 550-02) would have the 1500 Super engine and removable hardtop. In their early races the cars finished high in their 1,500cc class, including first place for the 550-01 at Nurburgring. Both cars won numerous events

in Europe, including hill climbs, and even went on to the Carrera Panamericana races—one winning its class and the other car retiring early. The only other Porsche to finish in this class was a stock Porsche 356.

This was the start of the true racing Porsches from Zuffenhausen. Under the direction of Ernst Fuhrmann, who years later became the president of Porsche, a new fourcam, air-cooled engine was developed. (Earlier engines had been in the pushrod configuration.) This new engine design became one of the most successful developments in motor racing. The car was a full-fledged competition racer and was shown at the Paris Salon in 1953, with production racing Porsches not seen until 1954. The limited

Top: *A beautifully restored Porsche 550 Spyder. Although it was not meant to be used, the convertible top was required for European endurance racers. Bottom: The cockpit of a Type 550. The painted tubes of the frame can be seen at the sides and bottom. Typical of a race car, there are just enough gauges and controls to get the job done.*

production run of the 550/1500RS also became known as the Spyder or 550 Spyder. The price for a light aluminum alloy Spyder in 1955 was about twice the price of a standard street Porsche. The RS designation translates to *Rennsport,* or "racing sports." About one hundred units were produced before the updated 550A/1500RS was seen in 1956.

Racing provided the attention and publicity necessary for Porsche to sell its street cars. As their racing successes continued, sales followed. Porsche always raced in Europe in any competition available, but it never officially raced in North America in those early days. One reason was the financial obligation, and the other was

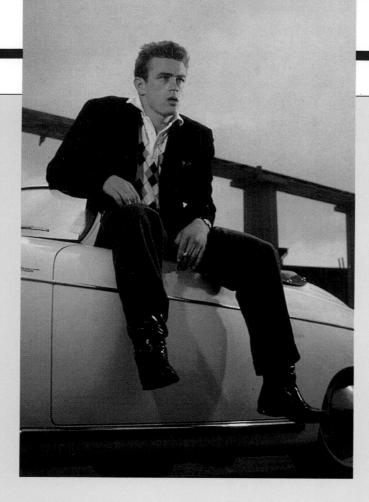

Top left: *James Dean sitting on the door of his 1955 Speedster.* **Bottom right:** *James Dean before leaving for the Salinas sports races on September 30, 1955, in his 550 Spyder.*

for the new 550. When the car arrived in early September, there was not much time before an upcoming sports car race in Salinas, California, so Dean drove the car around the Hollywood hills to accumulate mileage.

As the race day approached, Dean felt he needed more break-in mileage on the engine before redlining it on the track, so he chose to drive to the event, inviting along his mechanic, Rolf Wuetherich. But tragedy occurred at dusk on Route 466 near the community of Cholame: Dean's 550 collided with another vehicle at an intersection. His mechanic, though severely injured, lived, but only the legend of James Dean survives today.

Dean's Porsche 550 Spyder:
Shipped from Germany: July 15, 1955
Chassis No.: 550-0055
Engine No.: 90 059
Transmission No.: 10 146

Porsche 550 Spyders:
Facts: 75 customer cars were built
Chassis Numbers: 0016 to 0090
Today: Porsche 550 Spyders can be seen in historic races and some automotive museums

The Legend of James Dean

James Dean was a quiet, reserved man. At only twenty-four years old, he was achieving greater and greater success in the acting world. At the time of his death on September 30, 1955, he was filming the movie *Giant* with Rock Hudson and Elizabeth Taylor.

Dean's street car was a Porsche Speedster, but he wanted to go even faster than that machine would take him. In 1955, like today, the police were not too happy to see anyone racing on the street, so the next best place to go fast was on a race track; the best fast car was a Porsche 550 Spyder. Dean made a deal with the local dealer, John von Newmann's Competition Motors in Hollywood, California, whereby he would turn in his Speedster and pay an additional $3,000

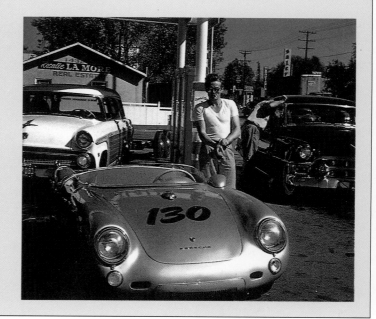

the distance from the factory in Germany. Fortunately, a group of amateur and semiprofessional drivers brought their own Porsches out to the tracks and raced with great success.

Besides winning races in Europe, Porsches began to turn up at events in the Bahamas, Guatemala, Brazil, and Mexico, as well as the United States, campaigned by private entrants. In early 1956, the Carrera, Porsche's new coupe, started racing in the United States. The 1957 sales literature stated that "the new Porsche series was proudly named for the Mexican road classic" (in reference to the Carrera Panamericana). The Carrera prototypes won first place in their class starting in 1954 and placed third overall.

By 1957, the 356A Carrera Speedsters with the GT (Grand Touring) engine in the 1,600cc class were the big winners. One of the most famous sports drivers of the day was Bruce Jennings in the four-cam Carrera GT Speedster, of which he owned three. The cars were all painted the same, ruby red with a silver nose, but with different suspension and gearing for particular courses —one for a short course, one medium, and one long. Bruce won more races with a Porsche from 1959 to 1969 than anyone in the world.

Porsche had some success with Formula II in Europe in 1957 and 1960. Privateers bought cars, rebuilt them, and at times even beat the factory teams. Each year the total number of Porsches seen in the winner's circle increased. By 1958 the 550 RS and the RSK were included, and the Carrera was collecting wins on both continents. In 1959, first (RSK), second (RS), third (Carrera), and fourth (Carrera) place awards were won at the Targa Florio. The next year an RS60 won.

The RS60 and RS61 were both built on a similar Type 718 chassis, the reason why you may sometimes see the car named after this chassis, such as 718-1500RS or 718-RS 60.

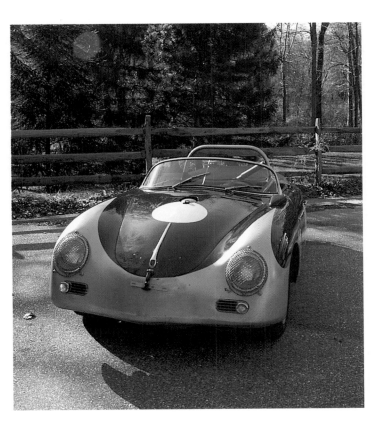

Left: *A well-preserved Carrera GT Speedster. This car was extensively and successfully campaigned in the 1960s by Bruce Jennings.*
Below: *This 1960 Porsche RS60 Spyder has spent most of its life running Pennsylvania Hillclimb Association events.*

By 1962, the RS Porsches were no longer competitive in the racing world, and during 1963 Porsche was working on the development of a new sports-racing car: the 904. Meanwhile, the chassis of the British car-maker, Elva, was combined with the Porsche engine to make an Elva-Porsche. These cars raced at the end of 1963 successfully and continued into 1964. Even today, it is not uncommon to find a Porsche engine combined with another manufacturer's chassis in a winning combination.

RACING THEN
Carrera GTS/904, 906, 907, 908, 909, and 910

Unveiled in November 1963 and officially known as the Carrera GTS, this fantastic Porsche rapidly became known as the 904; today it is rare for the Carrera designation to be used. A production run of one hundred cars was planned, with the first car delivered in 1964, but it appears that the factory delivered about 10 percent more cars to its customers. The factory offered this race car to the buyer as an out-of-the-box buy-and-drive deal. The body was made of fiberglass and bonded directly to the frame. The 904s were originally designed to have a 2.0-liter, 6-cylinder, air-cooled engine mounted in front of the rear axle, with a 5-speed gearbox, but development problems with this new 6-cylinder caused Porsche to resurrect the reliable 4-cylinder Carrera engine. A few later factory racing versions possessed 6- and even 8-cylinder engines. The Carrera GTS was considered one of the most outstanding models in the history of early Porsches.

The factory considered building an additional one hundred cars but decided against it because the next-generation racing model, the 906, was nearing completion. Officially called the Carrera 6, fifty identical cars

Type 904:
The Carrera GTS

Officially known as the Carrera GTS, this fantastic Porsche soon became known everywhere as the 904. The production run was planned for one hundred, with a second group of one hundred to be started when the first group was completed in April 1964. But the factory decided not to continue with the next group of 904s and to concentrate its efforts on the 906. (It is believed that as many as 10 percent more of the 904s were built using 6- and 8-cylinder engines, though no one is sure when these were produced.)

The early sales literature for the car was printed in German, but that did not stop the North American market from buying most of the cars. The Americans were excited about racing and wanted anything that Porsche could give them. Like the Spyder, RS, and RSK, this GTS was intended for sports competition; the brochure explained that "the purchaser is handed an impact-ready sports instrument." The 904 was also designed to be used on the street, was easy to drive, and even had a windshield wiper, but it contained very little room for a passenger, who had to rest his or her feet on a 12-volt battery. But by race-car standards, the accommodations were very luxurious.

The 904's 2.0-liter engine was directly behind the driver, with 185 horsepower at 7,000 rpm; it was an uprated four-cam Carrera. The rear bodywork could be rotated away from the cabin or could be removed as a unit. This was the first time that Porsche had used a fiberglass body, and it was bonded to the chassis, which was only 41¹/₂ inches (105 cm) from the ground and weighed only 1,350 pounds (613 kg) with no fuel in the 29-gallon (110-liter) tank. The top speed was 150 mph (241 kph), and it could go from 0 to 60 mph (96.5 kph) in 6.4 seconds and from 50 to 70 mph (80 to 113 kph) in 2.5 seconds—quite impressive for 1964.

The racing rules for manufacturing a car for the GT class were unusual: the passenger compartment had to be com-pletely furnished, the car had to have a full set of instru-ments, and the standard equipment, such as a spare tire, battery, and the large gas tank, all had to be fitted. Luggage space was also required, but since the size only had to be 65x40x20 cm, you were alright if you didn't mind putting your clothes in a box. There were many more require-ments, but the major rule was that at least one hundred identical examples had to have been built.

This car was designed to win. Today you may see a 904 at a vintage race, but more than likely one will show up at a car show. It is hard to believe this modern-looking car was designed and built in the 1960s. It is perhaps the most unique Porsche that Porsche ever built.

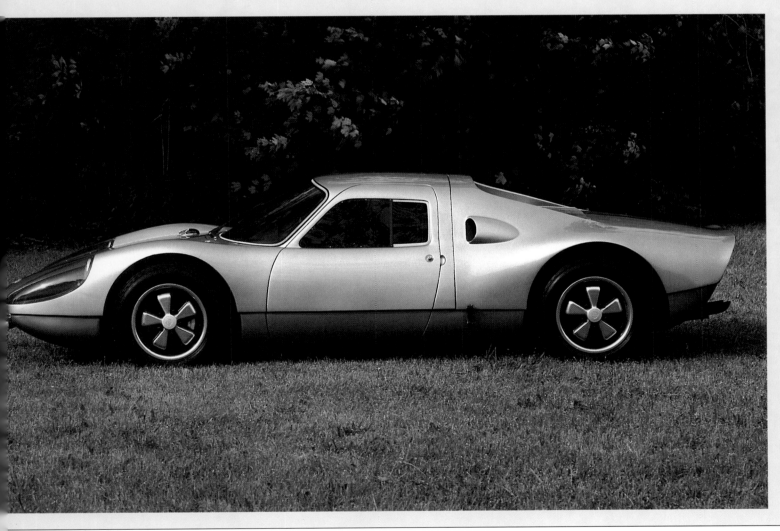

Opposite page: Initially named the Carrera GTS, the Porsche Type 904 race car is known by its number. Left: The Porsche Type 904 race car went from an idea to the prototype stage in only eight months. The fiberglass body is glued to the box-member frame, a concept that was patented. The air scoops cool the rear brakes. Fully race-prepared, it weighed 1,410 pounds (635 kg).

A restored Porsche Carrera 6, also known as a 906. These cars were offered for sale in early 1966 and were about fifty percent more expensive than the cost of a 904 less than two years earlier. With a fiberglass body and a tubular space frame, it weighed less than 1,400 pounds (630 kg).

with 6-cylinder engines (the racing version of the same engine that was designed for the latest street 911) were completed for the 1966 season to race in the Sports Car production class. A few other 906s were produced with various modifications, such as a 2.0-liter, 8-cylinder engine or fuel injection added to the six, that ended up racing in the prototype classification. The 906s finished successfully in races on both sides of the Atlantic Ocean, raced by the factory and by private entrants.

The man behind the racing department and the 906, the head of Porsche research and development, was Dr. Ferdinand Piëch, Dr. Ferry Porsche's nephew. The next big project to come out of Porsche was the 910, designed to be a factory prototype car not sold to private owners through 1967. Also during this time, the homologation rules changed for the Sports Car division, requiring only

twenty-five cars to be manufactured. The 910 automatically became eligible at the beginning of 1968.

The 907, a similar car except for its shape and right-hand drive, was under development at the same time as the 910, but it was not introduced until several months after. These cars, as well as the 909, were heavily raced in European hill climbs. The factory was always experimenting with gearbox changes, different suspensions, and lighter metals. A new 3.0-liter, 8-cylinder racing engine was developed for the 908 long-tail for endurance races and raced from 1968 through the mid-1970s.

Race fever had taken over the Porsche racing branch. The models 907, 908, 909, and 910 (Bergspyders) were developed at breakneck speeds and taken off to race by the factory racing team as soon as they were completed. Engines were designed with both 6 and 8 cylinders.

The 917, 917K, 917L, 917PA, 917/10, and 917/30

As discussed earlier, the official rules to homologate a car for racing required twenty-five vehicles to be built in one year. Though assembly of one engine for the 917 coupe took a total of 160 man-hours, the Porsche factory met the homologation requirement in 363 days.

The 917K was the short-tailed version designed for slower tracks. The 917L, tested for high-speed long straights, was 2 feet (60 cm) longer but had handling problems in poor weather.

The first overall win for Porsche at the famous 24-Hours of Le Mans was in 1970 in a 917 (short-tail version); second went to a 917L; and third to a 908. Although Porsche had won in its class before, it had never before won the first-place overall trophy. It was a great triumph for the year that included the 24-Hours of Daytona (first and second), Brands Hatch (first, second, and third), Monza 1000 kms (first), Nürburgring and Targa Florio (first and second with 908s), Watkins Glen 6-Hours (first and second), and the Osterreichring (first). In three years of competition, from 1969 to 1971, the 917K won fifteen of the twenty-four World Championship races.

In mid-March 1969, Porsche introduced the new Type 917 race car at the Geneva Auto Show (this is the cover of the sales brochure). It debuted with a 4.5-liter, flat-12, 520-horsepower engine and weighed 2,050 pounds (923 kg) with fuel. Twenty cars were offered for sale.

Top: *A restored 917 at a vintage car race at Watkins Glen, New York, in autumn 1979.* Bottom: *Mark Donohue on his way to winning the 1973 Can-Am Championship in a 917/30KL, most likely the most powerful circuit racer ever built. Its turbocharged 5.4-liter, flat-12 engine developed 1,100 horsepower.*

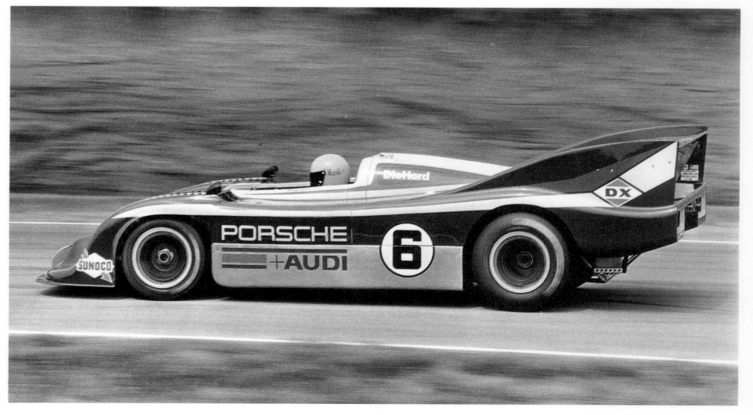

Volkswagen of America negotiated a special contract with Porsche AG to flagship a car for the Can-Am series (Canadian-American Challenge Cup Championship) that would use the name Porsche + Audi, the marketing company for the Porsche in the United States. The car was designed and built from a 917 coupe, with its top cut off, and used the designation 917PA for Porsche + Audi. The 917PA was never a very successful racer in 1969, and Porsche did not race in the series in 1970.

In 1971, the 917 ran in 5.0-liter form in the Can-Am series as a 917, and by 1972 it was turbocharged for the series, winning six out of eight races. The championship was taken by George Follmer driving the refined 917/10. This car led to the evolution of the 917/30KL, which made Mark Donohue famous and went on to win the 1973 Can-Am Championship. The 917 won a total of eight of eight races with Donohue, who came in first place in six. The car

was removed from racing due to regulation changes by 1975, but not before it made a closed course record at Talladega in Alabama in a 221.12-mph (355.85-kph) run driven by Donohue.

Carrera RSR, 935, and 936

Porsche developed the RS and RSR in late 1972. These cars looked like the 911 but with unusually large front air dams and protruding rear ducktails designed to provide the needed downforce to stabilize the car on the track. Two years later, the engine was turbocharged, and the rear had a more extreme whale tail. (Much of the turbocharging experience had been obtained from the 917s.) The 911-based Carrera RSRs were used as the development base for the 934s and 935s to come.

A 1974 Turbo Carrera race car. Its turbocharged 2.14-liter engine developed 490 horsepower. Handling improvements made on this car were later used in the 911 Turbo street cars.

Top: *Daytona 24-Hour, 1983. Porsche 935 No. 5, driven by Bob Akin, Dale Whittington, and John O'Steen, leads 935 No. 86, driven by Bruce Leven, Hurley Haywood, and Al Holbert, into the hairpin.*
Bottom: *An air hose connected to this 935 race car operates the on-board air jacks to raise the car.*

When the new 1976 regulations for the Group 5 World Championship of Makes were announced, Porsche decided to use the 930 Turbo as a base. The number designation 935 was picked. The rules allowed a "free" design of the front fenders, so the 911 look was replaced with a sloping hood with louvers above the front wheels. This look became a trademark of the 935 and became so popular that the Porsche factory offered a 935-type front-end option on a street 911SC.

The rear of the race car was a built-up standard Turbo spoiler, as required by the rules, with an adjustable rear edge. All rustproofing was removed and anything that would lighten the car was taken off. The front windshield was safety glass, but every other body piece was plastic.

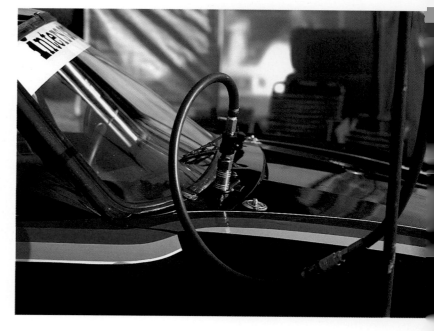

Anything that wasn't plastic was aluminum or titanium, and there was just one seat for the driver.

The racing awards earned by the 935 were numerous, including the World Championship of Makes and Sports Car World Championship and an overall win at Le Mans in 1979. The 935 continued to win high honors through 1982, with factory-sponsored cars as well as privateers winning thirteen victories that year.

The FIA organization (Federation Internationale de l'Automobile), in charge of worldwide racing, had been working on new regulations for the Group 6 sports racing class. These new regulations for racing took effect in 1976, and in that year both Group 5 and Group 6 raced together. The Porsche factory had been working on a new secret project that turned out to be the 936. Even though the number designation was close, it did not look anything like the 935. With the new regulations coming

into effect at this time, the 935 and the 936 ran together that year, with Porsche winning a double championship in both Group 5 and Group 6, adding another award-winning record for Porsche.

The time it took Porsche to develop the 936 was short. The parts were taken from existing proven race cars. The engine was from the 911 RSR Turbo Carrera; the chassis, transmission, and running gear were from the 917/30 Can-Am Spyder. The body design was a cross between the 917/10 Spyder and the 908 Spyder and had an aluminium space frame.

The 936 did not win its first race in 1976, but that was practically the only time. The 936 went on to win the 24-Hours of Le Mans, the World Sports Car, and Group 6 World Makes awards. By 1977, Porsche decided to cut back its factory racing teams and only ran in the Le Mans race, where the 936 took the win again. A private entry in

A 1977 Porsche 936 race car. This car underwent extensive but subtle changes from the 1976 version to reduce the aerodynamic drag. Power output from the 2.14-liter turbocharged 6-cylinder, taken from the 1974 Turbo Carrera, was about 525 horsepower. The car weighed just over 1,600 pounds (720 kg).

Top and bottom: *Details from a 1977 Porsche 936. Opposite page: At the Porsche test track near the town of Weissach, the 956s duplicate their 1-2-3 win at the 1982 Le Mans 24-Hour race.*

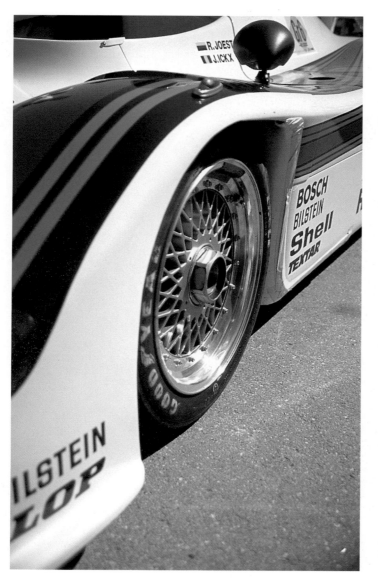

a 935 won Le Mans in 1979. The Porsche factory did not see the winner's circle at Le Mans again until 1981, this time with the 2.65-liter engine that had been developed for the Indianapolis 500 car that never ran, in the body of a 936, and with the four-speed transmission from the 917 Turbo Can-Am car. One of the drivers was Jacky Ickx, who celebrated his fifth win at Le Mans. It was the thirtieth year that Porsche had been involved with the French endurance race and also its fiftieth year as a company.

The Racing 924

In 1980, the 924 was racing in the SCCA (Sports Car Club of America) races across the United States, winning the SCCA D Production. By 1981, a new World Endurance Championship began. The 924 Carrera GT, based on the 924 Turbo, with a 4-cylinder, 2.0-liter engine with a turbocharger, was eligible to enter the endurance challenge (referred to as a GTR). Porsche entered three race-prepared cars in the Le Mans race that year, finishing sixth, twelfth, and thirteenth. The street version known as the Carrera GT, with a production run of four hundred cars, was sold out immediately. The Carrera GTS production run was only fifty cars, designed with racing equipment, and all were street legal in Germany.

The 956 and 962

Racing in North America in 1982 was centered around Porsche 935s in the SCCA Trans-Am and IMSA (International Motor Sports Association) Camel GT circuits. Porsche also wanted to enter the new Group C long-distance races. The rules allowed freedom of design, but each car had to meet a mileage restriction; the car had to be quick and fuel-efficient. The car designed by the engineers was the prototype 956. Not only did this new car

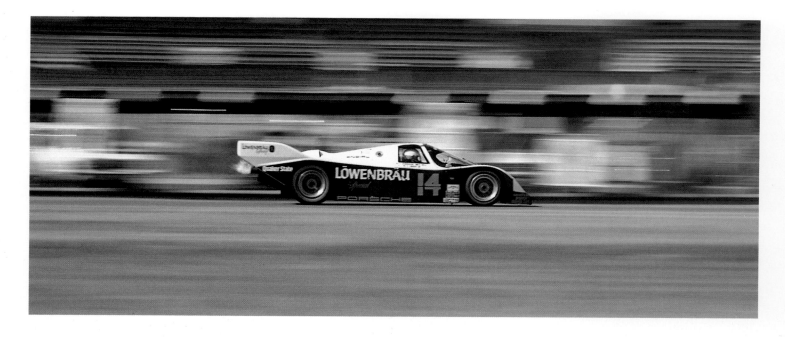

Top: Porsche 962 No. 14, raced by Holbert Racing, at Daytona in 1987. Bottom: Artwork sponsored by Löwenbräu to advertise their Porsche 962 entry in the Löwenbräu Grand Prix of Miami in 1986.

have an undefeated season, it won Le Mans in a one-two-three sweep.

The 956, and its successor, the 962C, won six straight Le Mans races from 1982 through 1987. The 956 used a twin-turbo, twin-ignition, water-cooled head from the 935 flat-six and evolved into a complete water-cooled engine. It started with a 2.6-liter engine and progressed to a 2.8-liter, 3.0-liter, and finally the 3.2-liter of today.

The 962 Up To Today

In 1984, the Porsche factory redesigned its 956 Group C Turbo coupe to meet the latest IMSA Camel GT safety regulations to race in North America. For the car to race in the GTP division, the chassis had to be changed so that the driver's feet were located behind the front axle line. The engine was also revised to a 2.8-liter, air-cooled, single-turbo, single-ignition, 934-based power plant. The new car was known as the 962 and also had design changes, such as an upgraded ignition and increased engine size. It continued to compete and chalk up wins through 1991.

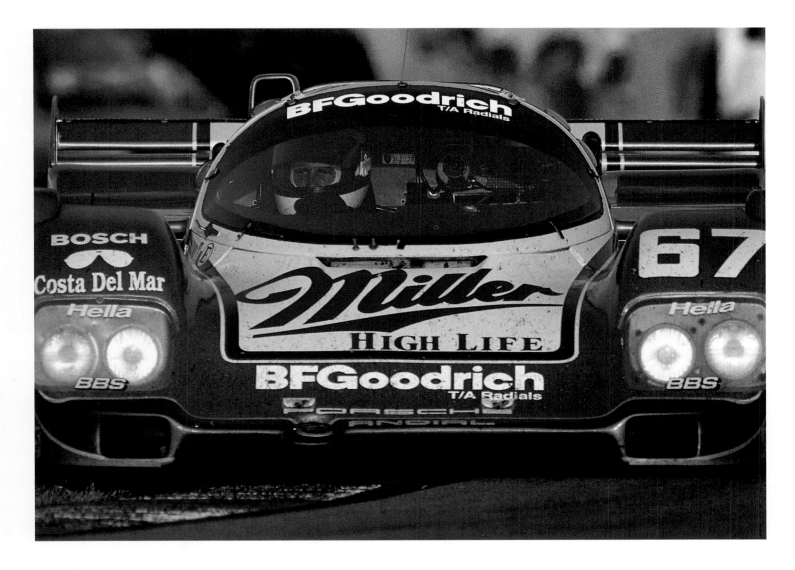

At the Daytona 24-Hour in 1989, the Porsche 962 No. 67 (chassis no. 962 108B), with drivers Derek Bell, John Andretti, and Bob Wollek, came in first overall. Following page: A side view of this car.

The first race of the 1991 IMSA Camel GT season in North America was the 24-Hours of Daytona, which takes place at the 3.56-mile (6-km) Daytona International Speedway road/trioval course in Florida. The winning car that year was the Blaupunkt Joest Racing Porsche 962C that was codriven by Hurley Haywood, Frank Jelinski, Henri Pescarolo, John Winter, and Bob Wollek—to a total of 2,559.64 miles (4,118 km) covered in the twenty-four hours. The closest finishing car was 64 miles (103 km) behind. This was the eighteenth time in twenty-three years of the event that a Porsche had won this endurance race. The most remarkable part of this win was that the 956/962/962C was from a ten-year-old design that had been winning races every year since it was first developed.

This victory was the 286th win for Porsche in the IMSA Camel GT Series. There is no other manufacturer that can claim even half as many victories.

Another record was broken at the Daytona race by Hurley Haywood. Tied with Jacky Ickx and Derek Bell for eight wins each in the international sports car endurance races, Hurley accumulated his ninth victory to date, all in Porsches. Since 1971, Hurley has won twenty-eight IMSA GT races and two IMSA GT Drivers Championships, and he has earned more IMSA points than any active driver on the Camel GT circuit.

In 1992, Porsche won four of seven races in the new IMSA Bridgestone Supercar Championship for street exotics, which gave Porsche enough points to win the Manufacturers Championship. Hurley Haywood became the first recipient of the Drivers Championship. The Brumos 911 Turbos, co-driven by Haywood and Hans Stuck, revived the classic paint scheme of the Brumos Porsches of the early 1970s.

The cars in the series, designated Supercars, included other exotics such as the Lotus Esprit Turbo, Dodge Stealth Turbo, Consulier, and the Corvette L-98. To equalize the competition a handicap was added: the more powerful the car, the more weight they were required to carry. All were lightly modified street stock high-performance cars and competed on Bridgestone Potenza street radial tires in short 30-minute sprint races.

decision was made to race two cars, using Teo Fabi in one and John Andretti in the other, so two cars had to be constructed. The March 90P chassis was given a 2.65-liter Porsche V–8 Indy engine.

The 1990 season was not very promising. Overall, the three-year Indy Program produced Porsche's first Indy Car victory and three pole positions with twenty-nine top-10 finishes. Porsche has not raced since 1990, and there are no guarantees for the future.

One of the original Indy cars, Foster's Quaker State Porsche, can now be seen at the Indianapolis Motor Speedway Hall of Fame Museum as an example of one of the most modern race cars that competed in the 500-mile (800-km) race. The ''Foster's'' part of the name derives from the Australian brewing company, a sponsor of the British Grand Prix and the Foster's Formula 1 Australian Grand Prix in November, the final race at the end of the Formula 1 season.

PORSCHE CARRERA CUP FOR 1992

The International Motor Sports Association (IMSA) has announced the newest race series for 1992 devoted exclusively to the Porsche 911, called The IMSA Porsche Carerra Cup. The new series is expected to run at least three seasons in the United States and Canada, based on the 1990 series in Germany, the 1991 German-based series, and a Carrera Cup Championship in France.

Vehicles raced will be identically constructed 1992 Porsche 911s powered by the Porsche 6-cylinder, air-cooled engine and sold through Porsche's U.S. racing arm, Porsche Motorsport North America. To ensure equal competition, all engines and transmissions will be sealed. No unauthorized preparation will be permitted.

Races will be run in conjunction with premier road racing events that already exist in the United States

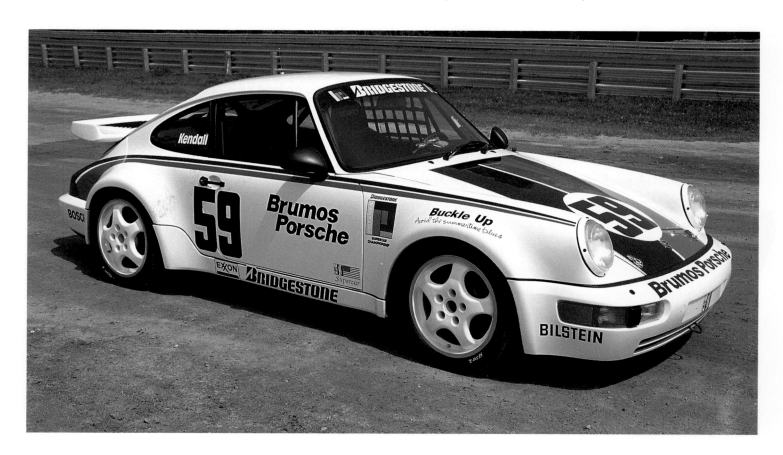

and Canada. As of this writing, eight sprint races are projected for each season.

RALLYING

Real racing is said to be the rally. Most endurance rally racing lasts days, through demanding terrain. In 1968, Vic Elford (now with the Porsche Owners Driving School), drove a 911 in the prestigious Monte Carlo Rally to a first-place win, the first overall victory for Porsche. Within the same month, Elford also won the 24-Hours of Daytona in a 907, the first overall victory for Porsche in a 24-hour race. His spectacular record has never been duplicated by another driver.

The most famous event today is the Paris to Dakar rally. (Dakar is located in Senegal, on the west coast of Africa.) Most of the two-week race takes place in the Sahara Desert. Porsche participated in 1984 with 92 other entrants; it entered three cars, coming in first, sixth, and twenty-sixth place. The Porsches entered were four-wheel-drive Carrera 911s. In 1986 Porsche entered the rally again, this time with the new 959 in rally trim, and won the race again. Porsche has not engaged in any official factory-sponsored rallying since 1986.

OTHER PORSCHE RACING
Amateur Racing

The SCCA has races almost every weekend throughout the United States during the spring and summer months, ending with a final week-long championship event in October at Road Atlanta, Georgia. These races, both for regional and national points, are designed for the fun of racing. The drivers are amateur racers, some of whom are hoping for the big break into professional racing;

This signed lithograph by Nicholas A. Watts is titled Paris–Dakar Rally 1986.

Hotline

For the latest North American Porsche racing news, you can call the Porsche Motorsport telephone hotline at (702) 348–3962.

others have been racing for over twenty-five years. Actor Paul Newman races in these events, mostly in Pennsylvania and in his home state of Connecticut.

Off-Road Racing

Porsche power is found in many places, including the SCORE/HDRA Off-Road World Championship events. Porsche teams won six of the top-seven finishing positions in the 1991 344-mile (553-km) Parker 400 in Parker, Arizona. The first-place 911-powered Chenowth race car was driven by Jim Smith over the desert off-road course. This was the only overall Porsche win for the season in this series, which contains eight other races until the finale at the Mexico's Baja 1000 in November.

VINTAGE AND HISTORIC RACING

Anyone can go to a race, even a race that features vintage and historic racing cars, and almost anyone can race one of these cars—even on a limited budget. There are more than one hundred vintage events a year in North America alone, and when you add in the United Kingdom, all of Europe, and the "down under" groups,

In 1959, Belgian grand prix driver Jean Behra had this single-seater race car created from a 1958 RSK. It has been restored and presently resides in the United States.

the count continues to multiply. Each group has its own rules for classifying an eligible vehicle, so to become a participant you will have to do some investigating; if you are a first-time racing enthusiast, you can, at least, get a sense of the basic requirements. If you look back at the early racing part of this chapter, you will be surprised to find that many of these cars are now racing in vintage and historic events.

Vintage and historic racing is a sport; it is not professional racing. There are at least two types of vintage racers: drivers who want only to take their cars on the track and bring them up to speed; and those who want to go to the edge, the max, of both car and driver.

Vintage and historic racing is part social and part competitive. This type of racing is designed for the friendly. The cars are carefully prepared for safety and the attitude of the driver should be the same. There definitely is wheel-to-wheel competition, but the main purpose is to have fun. Drivers do not want to hurt their vehicles or themselves.

The differences between vintage and historic can get complicated, with the size of the engine determining what group the car will be racing in. Some clubs may classify cars in different ways, but basically pre-war, post-war, production cars, and sports racers built before 1963 are in the vintage category. There is a separate classification that includes all Formula cars (Junior, Vee, Formula I, II, and III, and Formula Ford) built before 1969. Some associations classify these cars through 1963. The historic class includes production cars and prototype and race cars built between 1960 and 1973, with some overlap depending on the size of the engine. The only way to really tell what car is in what class is to buy a program at the event you are attending. The cars will be classified for each race.

There is a general conduct "13/13" rule that drivers are subject to: if you are at fault in an incident that causes

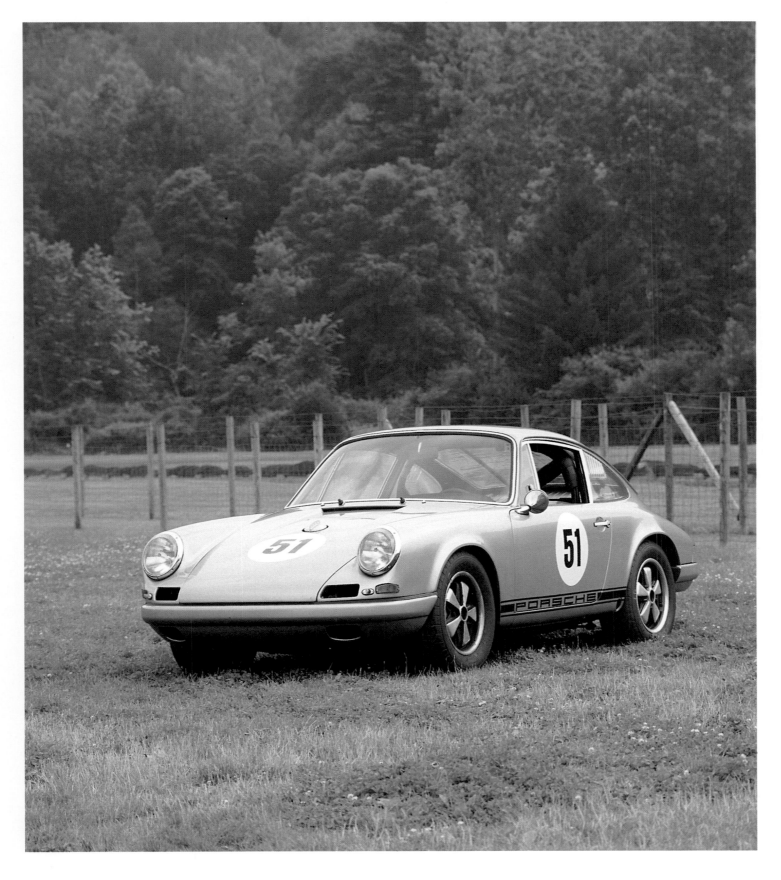

Left: *The 1967 911R was a lightweight 911 (1,810 pounds [815 kg], dry) with a slightly modified 210-horsepower Carrera 6 engine. The fenders, bumpers, doors, and lids were fiberglass. Only twenty-three of these were built; plans for a run of five hundred were abandoned due to the economy of that time. Following page: A 1966 Porsche Carrera 6, also known as a 906, next to a 1967 Porsche 910 (right). It is very difficult to distinguish between these two models. This photograph illustrates some key points where they differ: the shape of the headlight covers, the air scoops, and the center-lock wheels, which debuted on the 910.*

Participants in Concours
d'Elegance events can spend
hours making sure all parts
of their cars shine.

The Concours d'Elegance

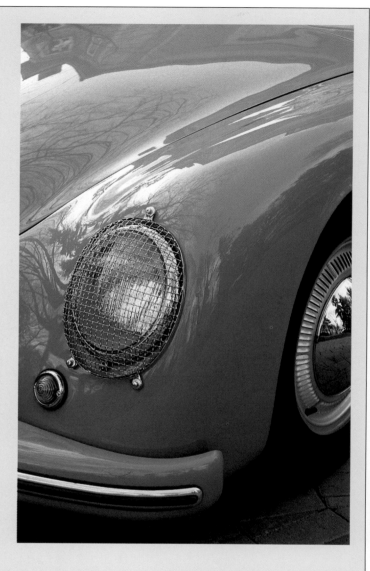

con-cours (kon-koor′) n. French. 1. moving together;
gathering. 2. competition.
el-e-gance (el′e-gans) n. French. 1. the quality of being
elegant. 2. anything elegant.

The above definitions could describe the Concours d'Elegance events, which began when automobiles were first
being exhibited in Europe prior to World War I. These
exhibits were displays of objects of art rather than performance events. In the early days both the occupants and the
machine were on display and judged as a complete package. Today only the automobile is judged.

The judging is based on the best preparation, restoration,
maintenance, and originality of the cars. Each organization conducting an event will have its own rules. The
automobiles are divided into categories: by age, sometimes by marque, and by a classification that could
include the quantity built. Depending on the total number of entrants, the designated categories are then broken
down by exterior, interior, engine compartment, storage
compartment (trunk), and undercarriage. Groups of
judges scrutinize every car and give points for each sec-
tion of the automobile they judge. Points can be taken
away for dirt and imperfections.

When all the points are added up, an award is given for
the best in each division. Then these first-placed winners
are rejudged to determine the Best of Show.

Receiving the highest award in a national show can add
to the resale value of the automobile.

Most devoted car lovers show their Porsches at least once
in the car's life. There are a few event regulars who become
obsessed with cleaning and shining every nut and bolt. Why
would anyone spend so many hours just for points? There is
no complete answer to this question. Some do it to relax,
some to see old friends at the events, some even to get out of
the house; each person has his or her own reasons.

To find out about events, you should watch the papers or
call local car clubs. Events can be local with individual car
clubs or a full international collection, such as the Pebble
Beach, California, Concours d'Elegance each August on
the eighteenth hole of the green overlooking the bay. The
cars are entered by invitation only, but the event is open to
the casual observer.

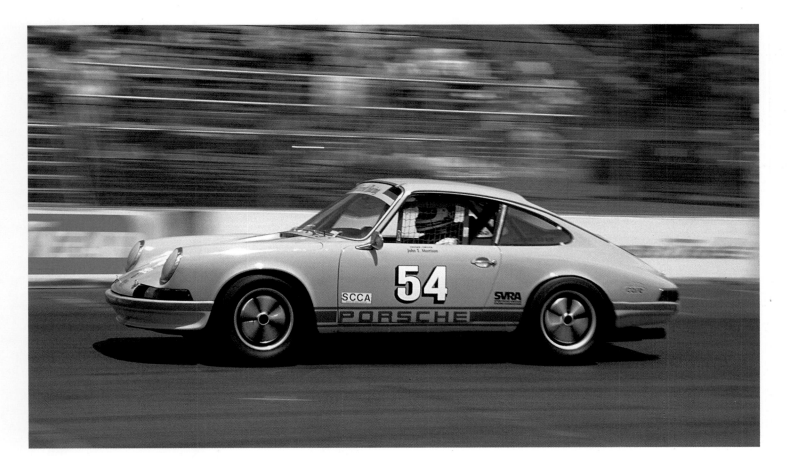

A 1967 911, which is still seen on the race tracks of North America. The car is old enough to run also in vintage car races.

damage to your car or anyone else's car, you are out of that event and on probation for thirteen months. Any further incidents while on probation will result in suspension for thirteen months. Any car involved in a crash, or having contact with another car sufficient to produce body, frame, or suspension damage, is automatically withdrawn from the event. (This rule does not apply to all vintage organizations.)

The greatest advantage of this type of racing is that it is usually a family affair. When going to an event to watch, you can bring everyone along, walk around the pit area, and look at the cars being prepared.

At some events there is an extra charge in addition to your entry ticket to get into the paddock area, but it is worth the price. Don't forget your camera. You will see cars that you have never seen before, and some you possibly have never even heard of. You will always see Porsches

at these races. Vintage and historic events can give the spectator the feeling of stepping back in time to the late 1950s when these cars were the latest and fastest.

It is easy to find out what track is closest to you. Publications that are helpful to consult are: *Victory Lane*, a monthly magazine based in Palo Alto, California; *Vintage Motorsport*, a bimonthly from Lakeland, Florida; *Grassroots Motorsports*, from Daytona, Florida; *Sports Car World*, from Lindfield, NSW, Australia; *Classic and Sports Car*, from Teddington, England; and *British Car*, from Canoga Park, California.

A few non-Porsche cars you may want to look for around the track are: Scarab, Chaparral, Ford GT, Cobra, Ferrari, Lotus, MG, Birdcage Maserati, Aston-Martin, AMC Javelin, Triumph, Austin-Healey Sprite, and Allard. You might find a Monsterati, Giaur, Peerless LM, Taraschi F-Jr., or Ginetta G4. See you at the races.

CHAPTER EIGHT

A PARTNER IN MOTORING PLEASURE

THE PORSCHE MYSTIQUE

A true Porsche fanatic fits into the space between the world as it is and the mystical. It is a way of life; it can continue throughout a person's life or only stay with him or her as long as he or she owns the car. It is a wonderful attitude, a point of view, a steadfast faith, and even a warm feeling all over. A true car lover understands this motto, this feeling.

To own a Porsche is an experience whether the car is brand new, direct from the showroom floor, or a previously owned model. There is nothing to compare to owning a sports car like the Porsche. No other marque is engineered like the Porsche. The Weissach engineers call it the leading edge. It has heritage, breeding, and a special elegance.

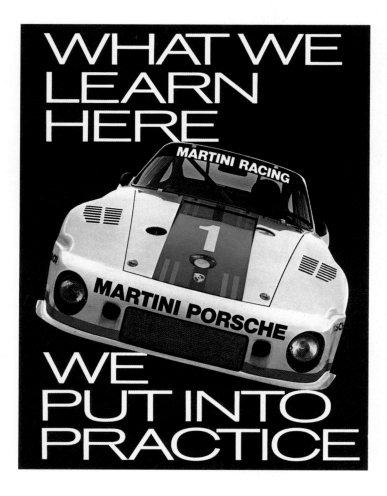

No other automobile company has had a history of as many accomplishments, has advanced the newest technology, won as many races, or continued its dedication to its customers as Porsche has done. First-time Porsche buyers may not even know about any of these factors at the time they are buying their cars. The first-time Porsche buyer may have wanted this automobile since a very young age, may have always talked of owning such a car, and now the time has come to take delivery.

The excitement may be hidden. The feeling may not show for days. But just let someone try to borrow it, and all that hidden apprehension of loss comes flooding through to the new Porsche owner. Of course, it is insured, of course, they will take good care of it, of course! The new Porsche owner would rather lend out the children then lend out the car. And, yes, it does come back in good shape, but that strange feeling of attachment has added to the mystique of owning a Porsche. There is nothing that quite compares to owning a Porsche and in many cases, many Porsches.

PORSCHE CLUBS

After you have taken delivery of your Porsche and have had some time to get acquainted, you may be ready to join a club. There are many advantages of a Porsche club membership, and they start with other Porsche owners. The Porsche Club of America is the largest independent single marque sports car club in the world. It began when a group of Porsche owners held their first meeting in 1955 to exchange ideas on maintaining their cars. They called them "gripe sessions," because it was difficult to get replacement parts and tires to fit correctly in the 1950s. Each owner had his or her own resources, and this was a great way of sharing. Through one of those sessions, for example, one car owner found out that

A 1959 GT Speedster.

Sears carried motorcycle tires that would fit the 356, which were less expensive than ordering from Germany.

By its twenty-fifth anniversary in 1980, the Porsche Club of America had grown into more than 108 regions throughout the continental United States, Alaska, Hawaii, Canada, and Germany. The total membership was over 14,000. Today, there are over 20,000 members in more than 125 regions of the world.

The objectives have stayed the same since that first day. It remains a group that shares friendship, goodwill, and the joy of owning a Porsche. The club provides many benefits for the Porsche owner. (Yes, you do have to own a Porsche and be at least eighteen years old.) One of the most beneficial elements of becoming a member is the monthly magazine, *Porsche Panorama*, containing technical how-to articles, racing news, restoration tips, and the latest new model introductions. There is always information on local and national activities and pages and pages of ''For Sale'' and ''Wanted'' sections for cars, parts, and pieces.

The individual local regions across North America have extensive activities including rallies, autocrosses, slaloms, gymkhanas, concours d'elegance, time trials, driver's schools, autocross schools, rally schools, dinner meetings, cocktail parties, picnics, banquets, technical sessions, work sessions, tune-up sessions, and general entertainment. Each local region also has its own newsletter for local members.

Once a year the PCA stages its Porsche Parade. This week-long convention of Porsche enthusiasts is held each year in a different location, usually during the warm weather. Members come from all over the country and abroad. It is hosted by a volunteering region, and members participate in a range of activities, from driving events and technical activities to a full point concours d'elegance and a rally. Trophies are earned for individual events and door prizes are awarded each day. Porsche factory officials come to the parade to conduct seminars. Often the factory delegation includes a member of the Porsche family.

A collection of jacket patches from the Porsche factory and events sponsored by Porsche clubs.

When it is all added up, it is really a wonderful idea. A Porsche owner can just pick out what to be involved with and enjoy the ride.

For membership information in North America contact: PCA Executive Office, P.O. Box 10402, Alexandria, VA 22310, (703) 922-9300.

In Australia, contact:
Porsche Club of New South Wales
P.O. Box 183
Lindfield, NSW
Australia 2070

In other countries, contact the Porsche factory for the latest membership information:
Porsche Club Betreuung
Porschestrasse 15–17
D-7140 Ludwigsburg
Germany

356 Registry

Another club that is relatively small, with about 3,500 members, is the 356 Registry, whose primary interest centers on the early Porsches. The club's low-key weekends are designed around swap meets, concours, touring, and banquets. The club has a high participation level, with events called "Holidays," topped off by a swap meet. Venders can sell Porsche "stuff," but the best part is finding the missing piece of your car that you have needed for ten years.

For more information contact:
Roger Whitton
356 Registry, P.O. Box 356, DePere, WI 54115

19TH PORSCHE PARADE POCONO '74

30 YEARS PORSCHE PARADE 1985
COSTA MESA · CALIFORNIA
PCA · ZONE 8

PORSCHE PARADE 24
FOUNDING REGION POTOMAC
SILVER ANNIVERSARY 25 YEARS PCA

1981 WEST COAST HOLIDAY V 356 REGISTRY

Aspen '78 COLORADO
TWENTY-THIRD PORSCHE PARADE

PORSCHE

17th PORSCHE PARADE CHICAGO REGION PCA

48 HOURS OF WATKINS GLEN 1981
PCA ZONE

PORSCHE

AUTOMOTIVE ART AND THE PORSCHE

What is automotive art? It is easy to state what it is *not*: automotive art is not the art of painting a flame job on the side of your Porsche! Automotive art is the image and form of the car, whether it be a racing scene or just the scaled-down automobile standing alone. The art piece can take many forms, from a sculpture in ceramic or wood to a painting in oils or watercolors to a serigraph. There are many types of automotive art today, available through special showings, advertisements in automotive magazines and newspapers, trackside art shows, or direct purchase from artists or dealers.

The earliest automotive art goes back to pre–World War I, when speed and mobility were associated with the excitement of the new motorcar. The art took the form of posters, commercial prints, stained glass, and even fine art including crystal figurines depicting the automobile. The medium had no boundaries; it sold to the automotive admirer.

Automotive artists include names we are very familiar with. Henri Toulouse-Lautrec (1864–1901) sketched the earliest automobiles, and after the war, the French artist F. Gordon Crosby (1885–1942) painted racing scenes from Le Mans. René Lalique's (1860–1945) first automotive work was in bronze and enamels, and later in glass. He became famous in Paris as a goldsmith and jeweller. Today, Lalique's original signed molded glass pieces of animals and women from radiator hood ornaments (car mascots) are very sought-after items. Even Henri Matisse (1869–1954) painted *La Route de Villacoublay* in 1917, a scene from the perspective of the backseat of a right-hand drive automobile.

Another artist who depicted the automobile was Ernest Montaut (1879–1909), whose technique gave his images a dramatic sense of speed. Other artists, such as René Vincent (1879–1936) and Geo Ham (Georges Hamel, 1900–1972) specialized in poster art. Many of their designs were used as illustrations for magazines and newspapers. Much of the time the drawings took the form of caricatures because of the amusing adventures that occurred during the early days of the motorcar.

In the 1920s and 1930s, much of the automotive art was seen in Europe, where sports racing was quite common. If there was a race going on, there were always artists sketching scenes to re-create the historical incident. Many of the poster pieces were used to advertise a specific event such as an exposition of the horseless carriage or an automobile club event. Of course, at that time none of this work was called fine art. None of it was shown in galleries or even hung in private homes as wall art. Most of these designs, sketches, or illustrations were, sadly, thrown away after the event or after being used to illustrate a newspaper article.

Also at this time, the art of decorating watch cases and penknives with a motoring theme became fashionable. Some of the early collectible pieces that have lasted over time started as awards that were given out for a particular racing event. These awards were made in bronze and sometimes ceramic, depicting a popular entry of the race. The art of collecting anything that has to do with the automobile can go on forever.

Many artists, such as Norman Rockwell (1894–1978) and Maxfield Parrish (1870–1966), did not specialize in the automobile but used the car frequently in their work. And as the motorcar became a household word, the automobile manufacturers used the art to sell their products. It was easy to stylize or exaggerate a painting of the latest automobile even before the product was manufactured. Even into the 1950s, Porsche sales literature used illustrations of the next year's models rather than photographs. By the time the cars were delivered, they did not always look much like the picture in the brochure. Finding these early sales brochures is a collectible art form by itself.

RICK COLE AUCTIONS

MONTEREY

VINTAGE SPORTS AND RACING CAR

AUCTION

DOUBLETREE HOTEL AT FISHERMAN'S WHARF

AUGUST 17, 18, 1990

A MAJOR BENEFIT FOR THE CHILDREN'S SERVICES CENTER OF MONTEREY COUNTY

Dennis Simon creates stylized images of classic sports and racing cars in his poster art. This image of a Porsche Carrera 6 was created for the Rick Cole Auction in Monterey, California, in 1990.

Since World War II, most of the automotive art has been shown for sale in the United States; many European artists have chosen to show their art in North America. The shows can be public or private, and if the work is racing-oriented, it is often seen at racetracks across the country. The latest hot market has turned out to be Japan. Many Japanese collectors are car lovers, who do not have the available garage space to own multiple vehicles; it is much easier for them to buy many pieces of automotive art.

Today, automotive fine art can also be seen for sale at famous auction houses before actual rare automobiles are brought up before the auction block. It is very difficult to estimate prices of new and old art; like other types of art, the price depends on the buyer at the moment of sale. An automotive enthusiast is well advised to buy what he or she likes, and not what he or she thinks may

appreciate in the next few years. Hang it in the garage, in the den, in the bedroom, even in the kitchen, but make sure to enjoy your investment.

Many kinds of automotive art are available to collect. Selective artists' works have been appreciating each year, and now that automotive art has been accepted by the public as "art," your likes and dislikes are the only thing that will hold you back. If you are on a limited budget, a poster can be acquired for a small amount of money; getting the artist to sign the poster will increase its value. If the poster is racing-oriented, another way to add to the value is to find the driver of the car that is shown in the poster or even the owner of the car and ask for his or her autograph.

For a little more money, one can acquire a limited edition poster or a lithograph that is signed and numbered. Sometimes the subject is an event; other times it can be a specific race or a specific automobile. The price range depends on the number printed and signed and the reputation of the artist.

After poster art, the range of work is unlimited. There are artists who specialize in bronze sculptures, such as Lawrence A. Braun, who casts in a very limited number by the lost-wax process. Braun's subjects can be the bust of a famous driver, an automobile creator, or a special car winning a race. Another artist who works in bronze is Stanley Wanlass, who often adds a hand-painted patina to his subject or presents his work in sterling silver. Wanlass often selects his models from his own collection of restored automobiles.

Another style of sculpture is created by Robert Hossack, who uses the Raku firing process, which creates a crackle finish with carbon highlights. Each sculpture of a classic or exotic automobile is unique in design and sometimes slightly exaggerated to create character in each of the pieces.

Another talented artist is Randy Owens, who is a master silkscreen printmaker. His original impressions (also called serigraphs) are very colorful and limited in edition size to about one hundred copies. Owens almost exclusively uses the race car as his subject. His images are also signed by the race drivers who have driven those machines.

The art of painting in gouache on paper has been perfected by the German artist Walter Gotschke. His work is deceptively impressionistic; the subject matter ranges from hill-climb racing of the 1950s through the cars of the 1990s, with each scene telling a story.

Another artist living in Germany is Carlo Demand, whose automobile art can be seen in six books that he has illustrated. The latest, *Porsche Renngeschichte In Bildern*, is all Porsche-related.

A few other names of artists whose work you can look for when auto art collecting are: Jesse Alexander, Harold Cleworth, Ken Dallison, Ken Eberts, Dave Friedman, Jerry Gambacinni, Peter Helck, Andreas Hentrich, Jack Juratovic, Jay Koka, Phyllis Krim, Sandra Leitzinger, David Lord, William Motta, Bill Neale, J. Paul Nesse, Charles Queener, Dennis Simon, Bill Stahl, Erich Strenger, and Michael Turner. There are also many more artists who are well known and greatly admired, such as Leo Bestgen, Paul Bracq, Melbourne Brindle, Dennis Brown, John Burgess, Sr., Dennis Fritz, Tom Hale, Dennis

Hoyt, Nicholas Watts, Nicola Wood, and Emanuel Zurini, in addition to many others.

The artists mentioned who are still selling their original works are relatively affordable. There is always a starting point—visit a gallery, go to a race, or even talk to the artist about his or her work. Some of these artists have illustrated books or may have books published about their art forms. There are lots of ways to collect. Even pages from old *Saturday Evening Post* magazines that are in frameable condition are sold at flea markets.

There are a few excellent galleries specializing in automotive items including original art, such as l'art et l'automobile in New York City. On the West Coast of the United States there is Crossroads Motoring Gallery in Carmel, California. In Canada you can visit Gallery Five Hundred Ltd. in Ontario; in British Columbia, there is Bob & Wally's Gallery of Automotive Art. One particularly interesting gallery, called Le Garage, is located in Tokyo and Kobe, Japan.

The exclusive Automotive Fine Arts Society produces a publication specializing in automotive art titled *AFAS (Automotive Fine Arts Society) Quarterly*. To inquire about a subscription, contact: GP/Publishing Inc., P.O. Box 325, Lake Orion, MI 48361–0325. The magazine features members as well as independent artists, and the organization sponsors one show a year in Pebble Beach, California, during the famous Concours d'Elegance in August. Many of the artists are in attendance, so you have the opportunity to ask questions and talk with them about their creations. During the same weekend there is also the Laguna Seca Historic Race, where you get the opportunity to see the early cars that the artists have used in their works of art. You can also see displays by individual artists at many of the CART and Formula 1 races from the Meadowlands in New Jersey to Adelaide, Australia. So enjoy hunting for that treasured piece of art celebrating the joy of car watching.

Coca-Cola serigraph by Randy Owens. Available in a limited issue of ninety-five prints, with forty signed by the drivers Bob Akin, Hans Stuck, and Jo Gartner.

Porsche Owners Driving School: "Driving in its Purest Form"

Now you have bought your car. You have been driving around, visiting friends, driving around, going shopping, driving around, stopping again at friends to see if they are home, driving around; you consider visiting your mother, but you continue to drive around.

But there is something new and different you can do with your car. Porsche has started a school for the new Porsche owner, located at this time in eleven different parts of the United States at eleven different times of the year. The schools are held at racetracks or parking lot locations and last a full day. (Porsche is considering starting similar schools in other parts of the world.)

The school is designed to polish driving skills and teach the new owner how to understand the potential of this high-performance automobile. The one-day school offers the unique opportunity to be taught by two Porsche racing champions: Derek Bell (five-time Le Mans winner) and Vic Elford (European Rally champion), as well as other instructors. This is not a racing school, but a school to teach precision driving, braking, shifting, and cornering techniques. You use your own car during these teaching exercises so that what you learn can be used in everyday driving situations.

After a great day of learning, it is all put together in a lapping session. You get to accelerate, shift, corner, and brake over a specially designed course. The instructors assess the smoothness of your driving and give you pointers on making improvements. There is also a session on the engineering and technical side of your Porsche to improve your understanding of the product you are now driving. In addition, a display of the latest models is offered; you have the opportunity to compare them and choose your favorite, with hands-on driving of each model through three different events: slalom, acceleration and braking, and roadability and handling.

In order to take the course, there are several criteria. You do have to own a Porsche (it does not have to be brand new) and provide it for the event. You must be eighteen years old. Yes, you must have a valid driver's license. You must also have a safety equipment inspection by an authorized dealer within thirty days or 1,000 miles (1,600 km) of the mileage on the car at the start of the school. There are a few more rules to read and waivers to sign, but the best advice is to go to a dealer for a brochure or call the school directly at 1-800-272-0999. It is a fun and definitely exciting day, which is why it is called "Driving in its Purest Form."

Bottom left: *Derek Bell describing a new driving technique to a Porsche owner at the Porsche Owners Driving School.*

APPENDIX

Galleries Specializing in Automotive Art and Other Motoring Goodies

Art & Automobile Ltd, Regalo 4–4 Natsugi-Cho, Nishinomiya 662, Japan

Automotive Emporium, 100F Turtle Creek Village, Dallas, TX 75219

Bob & Wally's Gallery of Automotive Art, 570 Clark Drive, Vancouver, British Columbia, Canada V5L 3H6

Car's The Star, 2450 Grand Avenue, Crown Center #202, Kansas City, MO 64108

Galerie Vitesse, 48 Rue de Berri, 75008 Paris, France

Gallery Automania, 304 East Street, Rochester, MI 48307

Gallery Five Hundred Ltd., 100 West Beaver Creek, Suite 13, Richmond Hill, Ontario, Canada L4B 1H4

Khachadourian Gallery, 60 Pall Mall, London, SW1 Y5HZ England

l'art et l'automobile, 120 East 34th Street, Penthouse G, New York, NY 10016

Le Garage, 5–17–1 Roppongi Minato-ku, Tokyo, 106, Japan

Le Garage, 4–1–14, Kaigandori, Chuo-ku, Kobe, 650, Japan

The Motorsport Collector, 5120 Bellmont Road, Suite S, Downers Grove, IL 60515

Crossroads Motoring Gallery, 169 Crossroads Boulevard, Carmel, CA 93923

The Scuderia, 1721 Lakeshore Road West, Mississauga, Ontario, Canada L5J 1J4

Many of the above locations include memorabilia such as mascots, books, posters, miniatures, sales literature, and inscribed photographs as well as original art.

BIBLIOGRAPHY

Batchelor, Dean. *Illustrated Porsche Buyers Guide.* Osceola, Wisconsin: Motorbooks International, 1982.

Clarke, R. M. comp. *Porsche 914, 1969–1983.* Cobham, Surrey, England: Reprint division, Brookland Book Distribution, Ltd., 1985.

Clarke, R. M., comp. *Porsche 924, 1975–1981.* Cobham, Surrey, England: Reprint division, Brookland Book Distribution, Ltd., 1982.

Cotton, Michael. *Porsche 924 and 944.* Huddersfield, West Yorkshire, England: The Amadeus Press Ltd., 1990.

Fujimoto, Akira, and Giancarlo Perini. *Porsche & Design, Car Styling Vol. 31 1/2.* Tokyo, Japan: San'ei Shobo Publishing, Co., Ltd., 1980.

Georgano, G. N., ed. *The Complete Encyclopedia of Motorcars.* New York: E. P. Dutton & Co., 1970.

Georgano, G. N., ed. *The Complete Encyclopedia of Motor Sport.* New York: Viking Press, Inc., 1971.

Grun, Bernard. *The Timetables of History.* New York: Simon and Schuster, 1979.

Harvey, Chris. *Great Marques: Porsche.* London, England: Octopus Books, Ltd., 1980.

Hindsdale, Peter. *The Fabulous Porsche 917.* South Laguna, California: Jonathan Thompson Publishing, 1972.

Jenkinson, Dennis. *Porsche 356.* London, England: Osprey Publishing Ltd., 1980.

Kimes, Beverly Rae. *The Star and the Laurel.* Montvale, New Jersey: Mercedes-Benz of North America, 1986.

Lewis, Lucinda. *Porsche: The Fine Art of the Sports Car.* San Diego, California: Thunder Bay Press, 1990.

Ludvigsen, Karl. *Porsche: Excellence Was Expected.* Princeton, New Jersey: Princeton Publishing, Inc., 1977.

McCarthy, Jim. *Vintage Racing!! Start to Finish*. Sparta, Wisconsin: RPM Enterprises Ltd., 1990.

Miller, Susann C. *Porsche 911, A Source Book 1974–84*. Baltimore, Maryland: Bookman Publishing, 1985.

Miller, Susann C. *Porsche 911/912, A Source Book 1963–73*. Baltimore, Maryland: Bookman Publishing, 1984.

Miller, Susann C. *Porsche Year 1982*. Laurel Hollow, New York: Carrera International, Inc. 1982.

Miller, Susann C. *Porsche Year 1983–84*. Clifton, Virginia: M&M Publishing, 1984.

Miller, Susann C. *Porsche Year 1985–86*. Clifton, Virginia: M&M Publishing, 1986.

Miller, Susann C., and Richard F. Merritt. *Porsche: Brochures and Sales Literature, A Source Book, 1948–1965*. Clifton, Virginia: M&M Publishing, 1985.

Porsche, Professor Dr. Ing.h.c. Ferry, and Gunther Molter. *Ferry Porsche: Cars Are My Life*. Northamptonshire, England: Patrick Stephens Ltd., 1989.

Sloniger, Jerry. *Porsche 924–944–928: The New Generation*. London England: Osprey Publishing Ltd., 1981.

Sloniger, Jerry. *Porsche, the 4-Cylinder, 4-Cam Sports & Racing Cars*. Reno, Nevada: db publications, 1977.

Strache, Dr. Wolfe, comp. *100 Years of Porsche Mirrored in Contemporary History*. Stuttgart, Germany: Dr. Ing. h.c.F. Porsche AG, 1975.

Tubbs, D. B. *Art and the Automobile*. New York, New York: Grosset & Dunlap, 1978.

Weitmann, Julius, and Rico Steinemann. *Project 928*. Stuttgart, Germany: Motorbuch Verlag, 1977.

PHOTOGRAPHY CREDITS:

Courtesy l'art et l'automobile gallery, ltd., New York pp. 131

© Christopher Bain pp. 30, 31

© Frank S. Balthis pp. 33

Courtesy Larry Braun pp. 148, 149

Courtesy B. F. Goodrich Tire Company pp. 104, 124–125

© Donna T. Johnson pp. 144, 145, 150, 152

Courtesy Collection of Tim Kuser pp. 68, 70, 72, 73

© Dominick Miliano pp. 1, 4, 25, 39, 40, 58, 65, 67, 70, 76, 80–81, 83, 90, 99, 109, 113, 133, 134–135, 138, 141

© Jason Miller pp. 52, 88

© Susann Miller pp. 6, 9, 13, 15, 21, 23, 24, 28, 29, 32, 34, 37, 41, 43, 44, 78, 90, 91, 94, 111, 112, 114, 116, 118, 126, 132, 154

© Ralph Morang pp. 52

© Leslie O'Shaughnessy pp. 86, 87

Courtesy Porsche AG pp. 8, 10, 11, 12, 13, 14, 15, 16, 17, 18, 19, 22, 26–27, 35, 36, 42, 46, 47, 50, 51, 61, 68, 69, 70, 72, 73, 74, 77, 79, 80, 84, 88–89, 92, 93, 95, 98, 116, 117, 121; photos © Rolf Frei 48, 66; photos © Klaus Reichert 53, 54

Courtesy Porsche Cars North America, Inc. pp. 55, 57, 62, 63, 64, 82, 96, 101, 102, 103

Courtesy Collection of Paul Rettig pp. 26–27

© D. Randy Riggs pp. 45, 56, 105, 109, 111, 119, 120, 130, 137, 139

© Ede Rothaus pp. 61

© John Shaw pp. 127

© Dennis Simon pp. 147, 149

© Bill Stahl pp. 61, 107, 118, 122, 123, 129

Courtesy Stanley Wanlass pp. 151

INDEX